WOOKWAN'S
KOREAN
TEMPLE FOOD

ILJUMUN: As the very first gateway one walks through
as you enter a Korean Buddhist temple, the Iljumun symbolizes unity
of the heart and mind as you walk the path of enlightenment.
**With open gracious hearts and peaceful minds,
let us humbly enter into the world of Mahayana!**

THE ROAD TO THE TASTE OF ENLIGHTENMENT

WOOKWAN'S
KOREAN
TEMPLE FOOD

WOOKWAN

PHOTOGRAPHY BY DUKGWAN MOON

icp international contents plaform

ICP Inc.
www.icphub.com

Distributor in Asia
ArtCloud9 Inc.
www.artcloud9.com

For information about special discounts for bulk purchases, please contact ICP Inc. at biz@icphub.com.

Book design by Kuki Hee-Yeon Sohn, SRC&C
Food styling by Wookwan
Recipes edited by Wookwan, Youngsun Lee
Contents edited by Mickey Yoon-Jung Hyun

ISBN: 978-1-7321914-0-2 (hardcover)
ISBN: 978-1-7321914-1-9 (ebook)

Printed in South Korea

10 9 8 7 6 5 4 3 2

First Edition

I am grateful for the Three Jewels,
Buddha, Dharma, and Sangha, for their mercy,

I am grateful for all those connected with
the Mahayana for their righteousness,

I am grateful for all sentient beings for their grace.

CONTENTS

PART 3.
WOOKWAN'S TASTE OF HARMONY
from coexistence of humans and nature

PART 4.
KNOW ONE, KNOW ALL
all life springs from the same root

PREFACE

Mahā (great, 大) is vast and boundless, encompassing all things,

Yāna (vehicle, 乘) is undertaking a long beauteous journey.

Gather beautiful connections;

The absolute (jin, 眞) and relative (sok, 俗), come together in harmony

Where azaleas bloom, the aroma of lotus leaf rice permeates,

In a place without worldly affairs, dishes and meals are plentiful.

Together, we will journey into the path of Mahāyāna (大乘).

In 2010, I had the opportunity to present an exhibition of Korean temple food sponsored by the Cultural Corps of Korean Buddhism. Throughout the duration of the event, I was moved by the level of keen interest and affection towards Korean temple food displayed by the audience, many of whom were leaders and influencers in New York City.

From this experience, especially as a practitioner of Buddhism, I felt compelled to take part in further advancing knowledge of Korean temple food to an international audience. Yet at the same time, I was also disheartened to learn that there were little to no available English works on Korean temple food when I visited several culinary institutions around the city. I thought to myself, "Once I return to Korea, I must work on an English manuscript on Korean temple food."

Soon thereafter, I found myself working with a publisher on an English manuscript and was over halfway completed. That was when I was invited by another publishing house to write a Korean version of a book on temple food. Due to the difficulty of simultaneously publishing two books, I decided to undertake the Korean version first, and I published "*Wookwan Sunim's Temple Food with a Mother's Touch.*"

At the time of publication, I did have some reservations, especially as a practitioner to publish a culinary work; therefore, thinking that the book may be the only one of its kind, I included as much content as possible. Fueled by the thought of it possibly being my final manuscript and with my passion to share as much as I could, the book ended up including over 230 temple food recipes in a single volume. The completed book was received with great positive response, and was praised as the most comprehensive of its kind in presenting temple food, for which I am most grateful.

As I continued to witness people growing increasingly accustomed to pre-packaged meals and fast foods, my thoughts began to evolve.

I thought I may never be able to publish another culinary manuscript, but did consider that in due course I might publish a book of poems interspersed with songs of understanding. However, as all existence is transient (諸行無常) and as there is no permanence in all living beings (諸法無我), my ideas too began to transform and reshape themselves. Meaningful considerations began to develop in me as I hoped to better the world and bring comfort to others by sharing knowledge of wholesome food culture and healthy ways of eating.

Around the time of the vernal equinox in the Dorak Mountains where I reside, sprouts peek their heads out from the soil, and buds begin to bloom. The abundantly flowering plants of the mountains are unlike those that can be seen in any urban setting.

The rising green embroidering all over the fields make my mind and heart grow rich and abundant, as if spring herself is greeting me with her warm smile. Even without going to the market, everything, found all over heaven and earth, becomes dishes and meals.

Whenever I am endowed with such blessings, I am in wonder of my providence and feel a sadness for those who are not as fortunate to have the opportunities to view and taste the same. Though I am sometimes able to share these gifts with those who visit during the time of spring, I often found myself wishing to be able to further share these these with others who had missed the blossoming of the new greens.

Throughout the course of the year, I traveled the mountains and fields, gathering and preparing all kinds of food ingredients, less those that may be poisonous. Encircling the perspective of monastic practices, I composed and published a book titled *"Wookwan Sunim's The Taste of Awakening."* The book gained critical acclaim and was praised to have opened a "new paradigm in temple food."

Many from abroad inquired about an English version of the book, and when finding there was none, strongly suggested publishing a translation. A number of publishing houses proposed issuing an English version, but none materialized, due perhaps due to timing. It wasn't until October of last year when Jeong K. Kim, President of Korean Buddhist Culture Services in New York, visited me and suggested publishing of a temple food book in English, that this current project was initiated. I am most thankful for his trust and passion for this book.

As this title is my first English publication to the world, it is comprised of an informative introduction to temple food. In due course, I hope to delve more deeply into the details and nuances of temple food by capturing the essences of spring, summer, autumn, and winter.

Today, we live in an open, connected world where various food ingredients are readily available. Particularly, in Part 3 of this book, Wookwan's Taste of Harmony, I hoped to embody the spirit of togetherness of the East and the West, as well as the interconnectedness with one being to another. I have illustrated simple methods of combining ingredients of the West and the fermented, natural spices of Korea.

Preparing and cooking food is not just about making ingredients delicious or pleasing to eat; it is a process of the preparer impacting the elements and components of the ingredients and carefully, mindfully connecting them, allowing each component to resonate with the heart, mind, and soul of the preparer. The outcome is that those who consume the food are not only able to nourish their bodies, but also nurture the spirit and soul. As such the case, I sincerely desire to spread this perspective of the unification of mind, body, and matter to all in the world who prepare food.

I sincerely hope and pray that by opening of this new chapter of connectivity through the world of Korean temple food, this book will may be embraced across the world and be beneficial to all.

Mahayeon Temple Food Cultural Center
January 2018

BALWOO: Balwoo is the term for the bowls used by
Buddhist monks and nuns. Literally, balwoo means,
"a bowl that holds exactly as much as needed," no more, no less.

WHAT IS KOREAN TEMPLE FOOD?

**TEMPLE FOOD IS A MINIMALISTIC AND NATURAL DIET
FOR PEOPLE WHO PRACTICE BUDDHISM.**

Korean temple food is built on the philosophy of Buddhism combined with a long tradition of Korean cuisine. From growing and gathering the ingredients to the preparation of the dishes, all steps are in line with nature. The resulting food does not only provide nutrition for a healthy body, but preparing the food is a practice of meditation as well.

Temple food is religious everyday food for Buddhist practitioners, but it is also food shared with all those who come to visit temples. By sharing this food, they also share their hearts and minds. In temple food, all or most of ingredients are either farmed or foraged from nature. It similar to what we call the "farm-to-table" process. However, since temple food is religious food, the entire process of farming, foraging, preparation, cooking, eating, and even cleaning, is considered as part of Buddhist practice and meditation.

With reverence for the wonders of nature and appreciation of the hard work of farmers, temple food is considered to be body and soul sustaining medicine. You eat only what your body needs so that there is minimal waste and environmental pollution.

KOREAN TEMPLE FOOD MAY BE THE BEST VEGETARIAN FOOD.

In temple food, no animal products are used except for milk and milk products. The reason for not consuming meat is from the Buddhist philosophy of generosity and mercy, a practice of not sacrificing a life for one's own survival.

There is also a restriction on using five pungent vegetables (green onions, garlic, chives, leeks, and onions). In Korean, these are called oh-shin-che, literally meaning "five spicy vegetables." It is believed that these five pungent vegetables, when cooked with heat, will lead your mind to have sexual desires, and when eaten raw, will bring anger into your mind. And so, these ingredients are forbidden for monks and nuns to minimize hindrances during their practice.

THREE PRINCIPLES
IN COOKING TEMPLE FOOD

In temple food, you prepare and serve each ingredient in a way that it retains its own natural characteristics and flavor. Preparing food with the three principles of clarity, flexibility, and compliance with the Buddha-Dharma, is considered to be a part of practicing mindfulness.

1. CLARITY

Clarity is very important in food because what we eat not only provides nutrients for the body, but also nourishes the soul. This is the reason why the one who provides the ingredients, the one who cooks the food, and one who consumes the food, must all have sincere and pure hearts and minds to achieve ultimate clarity in food.

Clean ingredients are able to purify our beings, therefore, using organic products that have been grown without any chemicals or genetic modifications is a good starting point of achieving clarity. Using only natural seasonings to obtain and retain each ingredient's own taste and flavor is of utmost importance.

Clean cooking starts with the genuine heart of those who are preparing the food. As each dish is being made, making sure that each ingredients' distinct characteristics are showcased reflects true clarity in cooking.

Keeping a neat and cooking environment, including clean tools, dishes, and utensils, are also a part of creating clarity. Lastly, eating in clean place with a thankful heart is also important.

2. FLEXIBILITY

Flexibility is the ability to create harmony in any given situation and setting. Ingredients should be prepared differently depending on the condition, time, cooking environment, and person who will be eating the food.

The dish's size, texture, temperature, and complexity of flavors should all be decided according to the diet restrictions and preferences, age, and taste of the diner.

3. COMPLIANCE WITH BUDDHA-DHARMA

Compliance with Buddha-Dharma is to follow the natural order. This is based on Buddhist teaching that humans and nature are one, just as the body and mind are one. Therefore, everything must be done in a righteous way: from obtaining the ingredients to cooking, serving, and enjoying the food, and as it all returns back to nature.

In temple food preparation, one must consider each ingredient as a living being, so it must be handled with respect and care. It is also necessary not to pollute or harm nature in any of the processes, and to always have a humble, grateful heart.

GONGYANGGAN: The gongyanggan is the kitchen space in a temple where food is cooked. For larger-scale events members of the public work alongside nuns in preparation.

CHARACTERISTICS OF KOREAN TEMPLE FOOD

Korea has four distinct seasons, so Korean temple food has developed a variety of methods to preserve and store seasonal foods during even the coldest of winter seasons. By utilizing the following methods, food can be stored or preserved for a very long time without destroying its nutritional value.

DRYING METHOD

Drying is one of the very basic methods of preserving food. Depending on tenderness of the ingredients, the drying process is done by different methods: under direct or indirect sun, in the shade, blanched and dried, boiled and dried, or by many other techniques.

FERMENTING METHOD

In Korean temple food, there are many different methods of fermentation and varieties of fermented foods. With this technique, the health benefits of microorganisms used in the process as well as their byproducts enrich the nutritional content, and also builds up a deep umami taste. Fermented foods are wonderful sources of minerals and vitamins that help your body system to work more efficiently; studies show that such foods can help lower cholesterol levels, boost your body's ability to fight cancerous cells, and also help build a stronger immune system.

Foods such as cheese, yogurt, vinegar, wine, etc. are just a few examples of fermented foods from other cultures. In Korean cuisine, fermentation is used to create some of the main basic sauces like doenjang (Korean soybean paste), ganjang (soy sauce) and gochujang (Korean red chili paste), and also in making pickled vegetables, kimchi, vinegar, and other extracts.

FERMENTATION METHODS BY USING SALT, VINEGAR, AND FERMENTED SAUCES AND PASTES

1. BRINING / CURING

Fermenting food by using mineral-rich natural sea salt allows food to retain its original flavors and fragrances during preservation. Depending on the level of saltiness and temperature, food can be stored for 3 years or longer. When ready to be used in cooking, wash and rinse according to desired saltiness.

2. PICKLING (VINEGAR)

Natural vinegar is a seasoning that has a sweet and sour umami flavor which preserves food well, and also helps the body digest more effectively by inducing the production of saliva and stomach acid. The benefits of vinegar enhance the qualities of the natural ingredients to create even healthier dishes. Vinegar is used widely in Korean foods like persimmon vinegar and Korean plum vinegar.

3. PICKLING BY USING FERMENTED SAUCES LIKE DOENJANG, GANJANG, AND GOCHUJANG

By using fermented sauces to pickle ingredients for further fermentation improves the absorption of nutrients in the body even more. This method neutralizes toxicity in certain ingredients to create both well-balanced and safe foods. Any ingredient can be pickled in this method, except for very toxic or poisonous ingredients.

4. KIMCHI

The word kimchi comes from the old language term, dimche, which means "salted vegetables." By salting ingredients, it draws out water, kills harmful bacteria, and activates good bacteria to produce beneficial minerals and vitamins to create a very flavorful and healthy kimchi. There are two basic types: one is using brine, which considered "white kimchi," and the other is "Korean red chili powder kimchi," which contains Korean red chili powder and other seasonings that activate the fermentation process. There are numerous kinds of kimchi that can be created by fermenting all sorts of leafy greens, stems, and roots.

5. EXTRACTS

Extracts are made by macerating ingredients in non-processed sugar or honey, as sugar causes microbacteria to ferment. During this process, multi-sugar structures becomes single-sugar structures which are more readily absorbed into our body when consumed. Extracts takes at least 3-4 years before it can be used in cooking. Many wild berries, sprouts, fruits, and roots can be used to make extracts that can be used as seasoning to produce a natural sweet flavor in cooking. Two or more extracts can also be blended to create an exciting complex layer of flavors. The most widely used extracts in Korean cuisine are made from Korean green plum and magnolia berries.

JANGDOKDAE: The jangdokdae is an outside space where many clay jars filled with different types of jang (ganjang, doenjang, gochujang) are placed for fermentation.
At the jangdokdae at Gameunsa Temple, there is a jar of ganjang that has been resting for over 10 years.

HISTORY OF TEMPLE FOOD

1. BIRTH AND EARLY ERA OF TEMPLE FOOD

Siddhartha, born as the prince of the Shakya clan, began what we know as Buddhism approximately 2500 years ago. In a well-known episode during his ascetic life, he became seriously ill during meditation due to starvation. A girl named Sujata offered him a creamy porridge made from fermented milk which allowed him to recover from his illness. This story illustrates what was to be the birth of temple food. During the early era, Buddhist monks went from house to house to gather offerings of food. As the monks found semi-permanent places to practice meditation during the three months of the wet season, their main diet consisted of dried cooked rice, mixed rice with beans and barley, ground up grains and rice cakes, and vegetables, flowers, fruits, milk, and honey as snacks.

During this time, the five pungent vegetables and meat were allowed to be used for the cure of illnesses. These exceptions are still practiced in countries like Thailand and Myanmar today.

2. HISTORY OF KOREAN TEMPLE FOOD

Buddhism was introduced to Korea during Three Kingdoms Era (Goguryeo, Baekje, and Silla) in the 4th century. In 372 AD, it was accepted by the King in Goguryeo and they also accepted by King of Baekje in 384 AD. During the 5th century, Goguryeo introduced Buddhism to Shilla, but was rejected by the nobility. It was finally accepted by King Beopheung when Chadon Lee, a prominent court official, was martyred in 527 AD.

The early years of Buddhism in Korea was developed and deeply rooted in the royal families and their attempts to strengthen their influence, which has in turn shaped Buddhism in modern and contemporary Korea.

During the Three Kingdoms Era, vegetarianism in Buddhist teachings influenced how the upper class ate, and even the food served in the royal court. As Buddhism became the state religion and began to grow in popularity during the Goryeo kingdom (918-1392 AD), so did the refinement in temple food by utilizing a wider variety of vegetables, vegetable oils, herbs, and spices.

Tea drinking was considered as a way to practice Buddhism, and so tea offerings to Buddha and to one's ancestors was widely practiced. Deep fried snacks made of flour, oil, and honey and convenient tea powders made from steamed tea leaves were also widely enjoyed.

In the Joseon Dynasty (1392-1910 AD), Confucianism and Daoism was adopted as the state religion and the influence of Buddhism started to diminish. However, temple food had already become deeply rooted in everyday life among commoners and monks. The temples deep in the mountains began to use ingredients found and farmed locally, and this early farm-to-table concept became the foundation of modern Korean temple food today.

Bori-gogae, or literally "barley hump," is a term coined for the period of time usually around May and June, when food is not enough because the crops harvested in the previous year has been exhausted and the harvest for the current year not yet ripe. During the Japanese occupation of Korea (1910-1945) and through the 1950s and 1960s following the Korean War, many people were impoverished. People had to be creative in finding and preserving edible foods; ingredients that were too tough to eat were tenderized by utilizing fermented sauces like Korean soybean paste, soy sauce, and Korean red chili paste. Nothing was wasted as food. People found ingenious ways to neutralize toxicity in poisonous ingredients to create safe foods to eat. Many different techniques and recipes were developed during this time and we still see them in today's Korean temple food cuisine.

COMMUNAL WORK (OOL YEOK):
Working together in harmony
with a caring and thankful heart.

STORY OF SEASONING

NATURAL SEASONING, CONSUMED AS MEDICINE AND USED AS MEDICINE

The words yang-nyeom meaning "seasoning" in Korean, was originated from two words: "yak," which means medicine, and "nyeom," which means thinking or thought. As shown in its origin, yang-nyeom was once used as medicine, and nowadays it is used to enhance the flavors of food.

It is essential that a food preparer involves his/her entire heart and mind into the food in order to create and serve the meal as medicine for the body and soul. What makes Korean temple food unique is that unlike regular food, five popular spices are not used, and any excessive use of yang-nyeom is avoided. This is also why it is so important that the nutrients of all the ingredients and within yang-nyeom are well preserved and retained as much as possible during food preparation.

Korean temple food must be prepared as if it is a good medicine to keep our body healthy, not just to satisfy our taste buds. By using fresh seasonal ingredients and yang-nyeom, the food will be more than a meal, but natural medicine for the soul.

TRADITIONAL "JANG"

"Jang" is the most basic and important seasoning used in Korean food.

DOENJANG (KOREAN SOYBEAN PASTE) AND GANJANG (KOREAN SOY SAUCE)

Doenjang and ganjang are fermented seasonings made of soybeans and has been used as main yang-nyeom for over 2000 years in Korea. The base of these two seasonings is meju; soybeans are harvested in the fall, then cooked and mashed into brick shapes in the early winter to make meju. Wrapped in rice straws, meju is fermented for two weeks in a warm place where they harden. The hardened meju bricks are then tied with rice straws to the eaves of homes for air-drying for two months. During this time, various bacteria such as Bacillus subtilis and Aspergillus oryzae (also known as koji), and lactic acid bacteria are naturally cultured.

Before spring, meju bricks are fermented in brine. After 40 to 60 days of fermentation, meju chunks are mashed to become doenjang while the filtered brine that is left over becomes ganjang. The process of fermentation increases the body absorption rate of proteins and other nutrients from the soybeans from 30% to over 90%. It takes more than two years of fermentation to make excellent doenjang and ganjang.

Doenjang

Ganjang

GOCHUJANG (KOREAN RED CHILI PASTE)

Gochujang is made from barley malt powder, meju powder, chili powder, and glutinous rice. It is a unique natural seasoning with complex flavors composed of the spiciness from chili, the sweetness from the starch of cooked glutinous rice, a savory taste from amino acids produced by the decomposition of soybean proteins, and the savoriness from salt. Gochujang's unique flavors are due to the organic acids like citric acid, lactic acid, acetic acid, and even alcohol that arise during the fermentation process as well as a distinct sweetness from the starch in the sweet rice and barley.

GOCHUJANG*

600 g Korean red chili powder, fine
1.2 L fruit or vegetable juice
100 g all-purpose flour
200 g coarse salt
200 ml water

1. Boil vegetable or fruit juice for about 1 hour in low heat.
2. Add flour to the water and boil for 10 minutes in low heat.
3. Combine 1 and 2 after boiling and when they are lukewarm, then add salt and stir well.
4. Add fine chili powder in 3 and stir well.
5. Put 4 in a sanitized glass jar and cover the top with cloth for ventilation.

* This recipe is a simplified version from the traditional method.

Gochujang

RICE SYRUP

Rice syrup is made by either boiling or steaming powdered grains to which malt (barley or other grain that has been steeped, germinated, and dried) and hot water is added. This mixture is then filtered with a hemp cloth and the liquid that is left, called yeot-mul, in boiled further in a big thick pot for a few hours until its thickness becomes like honey. Rice syrup enhances the sweetness in dishes and can even makes food look glossy. It can also be used to aid fermentation.

SALT

Salt is one of the most basic and important ingredients when cooking. It keeps the color of vegetables more vivid and helps retain their nutrition when added to water while boiling them. The flavor and aroma of pickled vegetables with salt can be readily preserved as well.

Sun-dried sea salt must be stored in shade for about three years, and it is better to use salt from natural extraction. It is best to melt the sea salt in water and to filter out the impurities before using in cooking. The best quality salts are the kinds baked in a bamboo, porcelain, or germanium container at temperatures over 1000°C.

Rice syrup   Fine salt

VEGETABLE STOCK,
A BASE SOUP OF ALL CUISINE

Vegetable stock is useful in all soup based cuisines. It can be used to cook rice or porridge, all kinds of vegetable dishes such as stir fried or boiled down vegetables, and even kimchi. It can be used in place of cooking oil which can lighten and enhance the flavors of the dish as well as make it easier for the body to digest.

VEGETABLE STOCK

1 L water
5 pieces dried shiitake mushroom
200 g Korean daikon radish
3 pieces dried kelp (10 cm x 10 cm)

1. Boil water with the mushrooms and radish for 20 minutes over medium heat.
2. Add kelp and boil for 7 more minutes to complete. Boiling times and ingredients used can be varied by occasion.
3. As a variation, boil the water with 10 pieces of shiitake mushrooms only for 2 hours to fully infuse the flavors, or 3 pieces of kelp (10 cm x 10 cm) only for hours.

Vegetable stock

NATURAL CONDIMENT

Natural condiments are powdered ingredients naturally dried or steamed then dried, which preserves their original nutrients.

NATURAL POWDER

Powdered pungent vegetables or spices can be used as yang-nyeom; not only are their flavors and aromas used, but their medicinal effects are much needed in winter when fresh food materials are rare. Natural powders promote digestion by stimulating the salivary gland, can neutralize gluten when mixed with flour, and their aromas have the ability to calm the nerves. It is good to use them in small amounts to enjoy their flavors.

FERMENTED EXTRACT

It is best to use seasonal fruits, or sprouts, leaves, and roots of wild vegetables to make fermented extracts. Sugar is added to those ingredients and fermented for a period of time, allowing enzymes with minerals and vitamins from the original ingredients to be extracted out.

At least three years of fermentation is needed for the liquid to be ready to be used as yang-nyeom. When the process is complete, the extract can be used in cooking instead of sugar. Since the microbes within the extract are active, it is best to use this ingredient in uncooked food rather than cooked food. In general, green plums, magnolia berries, raspberries, mulberries, and wild vegetables are good for making fermented extracts. These extracts can also be mixed in water to be made into cold or hot drinks.

FERMENTED GREEN PLUM EXTRACT

1. Add 3~4 kg of sugar to 10 kg of green plums and mix well.
2. Ferment for 3 to 4 days in room temperature until bubbles appear.
3. Add an additional 3 kg of sugar and mix well.
4. Put everything in a big jar and put 1 kg of sugar on the top and cover with cloth.
5. Place the jar in a shaded and cool area and avoid direct sunlight.
6. For the first three months, stir every 15 days for better fermentation.

The ratio of green plums to sugar is usually 1:1, but at the Mahayeon Temple Food Cultural Center, the ratio is 1:0.7. After a year, separate the chunks of green plums and ferment the extract only. The twice fermented extract can be used in drinks. For cooking, it is better to use the extract after three years of fermentation. All extracts can be made with the same process.

Fermented green plum extract

WATER

Water is the most important base in all cuisine. The quality and taste of food depend heavily on what kind of water is used in cooking. Using good water also helps to ferment better jang and can even enhance the flavors of dishes. When using tap water, it is recommended to filter or boil the water before use as it can contain chlorine and fluorine.

MEASUREMENT USED IN THIS BOOK:

1 tablespoon = 15 ml
1 teaspoon = 5 ml
1 cup = 200 ml

Since recipes in this book is based on the soy sauce, soybean paste, red chili paste made at the temple, the salinity of the ingredients may differ from the ones readers are using at home. Please adjust the amount of yang-nyeom according to your own tastes and health needs. The salt used in this book generally refers to sea salt that is coarse in texture, fine salt refers to fine-grain salt that has been baked at 1400°C.

* Please note that this book uses both U.S. and metric unit systems.

PART 1.

WOOKWAN'S
TASTE OF OFFERING

from a pure mind

RICE

RICE

Rice is the center of Korean food culture. It is the base of all Korean meals. If you have tasty rice, it is said that you won't even need any side dishes. If you cook rice with other ingredients together, it is as if you are cooking rice and the side dishes at the same time; for example, if you are having sticky rice wrapped with lotus leaves, the aroma from the lotus leaves acts as your side dish. If you are having white rice with assorted mushrooms, all you need is a seasoned soy sauce or red chili paste to go with the rice. In the temple, rice is offered to Buddha first, and then served to monks and others at the temple.

* Icheon, where I live, is famous for its delicious rice. It produces the best rice in all of Korea since it has the perfect natural surroundings and conditions for the crops: sufficient sunlight, ideal daily temperature differences during ripening season, and plentiful nourishment in the well-mixed clay and sand in the soil. From olden times, rice from Icheon was selected to be served to kings.

Yeonnip-bap

STICKY RICE WRAPPED IN LOTUS LEAF

the scent of lotus leaves radiates through the mind and body

———————

Serves 2-4
Preparation time:
1 hour 50 minutes
Cooking time: 30 minutes

2 lotus leaves
400 g sticky rice
16 ginkgo nuts, boiled for 3 minutes
12 dried lotus seeds, soaked in room temperature water for 10 minutes
2 tablespoons pine nuts
1/2 teaspoon fine salt, for washing lotus leaves

1. Wash and rinse the sticky rice. Soak in water for about 1 hour.
2. Cook sticky rice. Rice should be slightly al dente.
3. If using fresh lotus leaves, wash them in fine salt water and pat them dry.
   If using dried leaves, soak them in water until they are soft.
4. Place a lotus leaf on a plate. Place half of cooked rice in the center of the lotus leaf.
5. Arrange half the ginkgo nuts, lotus seeds, and pine nuts on top of rice.
6. Wrap the rice by folding the bottom side of the leaf over the rice, then folding the two sides of the leaf over the rice, and finally fold the top side of the leaf over the rice and tuck. Repeat steps 4~6 for the other lotus leaf.
7. Steam for 30 minutes, then serve on plates.

———————

Nutrients in lotus leaves are fully absorbed in the sticky rice and the essence of the leaves make the rice glossy with a distinct brown color. Lotus leaves picked in May and June are soft enough to eat, while matured leaves picked in July and August add more flavor and aroma to rice with their strong scent and plentiful nutrients, but are too tough to eat.

LOTUS LEAVES have numerous health benefits. They are high in iron and unsaturated fats, and can help prevent anemia and low blood pressure. It helps purify the blood and also promotes blood circulation. Lotus leaves also lower the body temperature and helps to calm the mind. In addition, lotus leaves have strong antimicrobial effects, making them an ideal vessel for food to stay fresh during the hottest of summer days. Lotus leaves can also be cured to be used as brewing tea.

MUSHROOMS are thought of as gifts from God. From ancient times, they were treasured ingredients for their many health benefits, as they have anti-aging properties and promote longevity. Mushrooms are also aromatic, tender, and deliver complex flavors. They are low in fat, high in fiber, and effective in improving vascular function and preventing constipation.

Modeum-beoseot-bap

WHITE RICE WITH ASSORTED MUSHROOMS

infused with the rich aroma and nutrients of mushrooms

Mushrooms that are freshly picked from nature have excellent flavors and aromas compared to the ones bought in stores. No matter which mushrooms you use, rice with assorted mushrooms alone serves as a complete meal with enough nourishment and flavors with no need for side dishes.

Serves 3-4
Preparation time: 1 hour
Cooking time: 30 minutes

1 cup short-grain white rice

15 g dried shiitake mushrooms

15 g dried white wood ear mushrooms

50 g king oyster mushrooms

50 g oyster mushrooms

50 g enoki mushrooms

1 tablespoon soy sauce

1 tablespoon perilla seed oil

2 cups water, for soaking dried mushrooms

SEASONED SOY SAUCE:
MIX ALL INGREDIENTS

1 teaspoon soy sauce

1 tablespoon perilla seed oil

1 tablespoon roasted sesame seeds

1 Korean green chili pepper, seeded and minced

1. Wash and rinse the rice. Soak in water for about 1 hour.
2. Rehydrate dried shiitake and dried white wood ear mushrooms by soaking them in water.
3. Save the water after soaking the mushrooms.
4. Cut off the stems of shiitake mushrooms and slice thinly.
5. Cut white wood ear mushrooms into small bite-sized pieces.
6. Slice king oyster mushrooms thinly.
7. Cut the bottom of enoki mushrooms, and tear it into thin pieces by hand. Tear oyster mushrooms by hand as well.
8. In a mixing bowl, add all mushrooms except the enoki mushrooms. Add soy sauce and perilla seed oil. Mix well.
9. In a pot, add rice and water from soaking the mushrooms. Add seasoned mushrooms on top.
10. Bring to a boil over high heat.
11. Reduce heat to low for about 10 minutes. Add the enoki mushrooms and cover for 1~2 minutes. Turn off heat.
12. Stir rice gently. Serve with seasoned soy sauce on the side.

PORRIDGES

PORRIDGES

Eating soft porridge in the morning improves the body's digestive functions and helps to energize the body. You can use grains along with various vegetables to make porridges. It is one of the best ways to cook vegetables since their nutrients can be absorbed most efficiently.

Daechu-yumi-juk

CREAMY JUJUBE PORRIDGE

boosts energy and fortifies the body

The sweetness of the jujubes and the soft, mild taste of milk harmonize with the brown rice in this creamy jujube porridge. This recipe, when used with the highest quality milk, reflects the one used for the porridge that was offered to Buddha right before his enlightenment. A Buddhist trainee starts his day with gratefulness, and a bowl of porridge as breakfast.

Serves 3-4
Preparation time: 4 hours
Cooking time: 25 minutes

1 cup short-grain brown rice
30 dried jujubes
3 cups water
3 cups milk
Fine salt to taste

1. Wash and rinse the brown rice. Soak in water for about 4 hours.
2. Grind the soaked brown rice in a blender with 1 cup of water until it becomes very fine in texture.
3. Puncture each jujube with the tip of a knife, and add them to a pot with 2 cups of water.
4. Bring to a boil, then reduce heat and simmer for 30 minutes.
5. Remove the pits from the jujubes. In a fine strainer, press down the jujubes to get a puree.
6. In a thick-bottomed heavy pot (or non-stick pot), add the jujube puree and ground brown rice.
7. In low heat, stir with a wooden spoon (or rubber spatula) while adding small amounts of milk until the rice is fully cooked with a porridge-like consistency.
8. Season with salt and serve.

JUJUBES (DATES) grown and harvested in the cold dew then dried off, are sweet, juicy, and high in nutrients. Jujubes help build a stronger stomach and spleen, and improves digestive functions. Eaten over time, jujubes can also reduce the discomforts of cold hands and feet, and quiets the nerves.

Sigeumchi-eunhaeng-jat-juk

SPINACH PORRIDGE WITH GINKGO NUT AND PINE NUT

filled with an embracing warmth that promotes a healthy body

Dark green vegetables like spinach are already plentiful in nutrients, but the pine nuts and ginkgo nuts in this porridge supplement their benefits even more. It has been a long standing tradition to have porridge as breakfast in the Buddhist temples and doing so appeases hunger, quenches thirst, helps digestion, and can even aid in preventing a stroke.

Serves 3-4
Preparation time:
1 hour 10 minutes
Cooking time: 20 minutes

1 cup short-grain white rice
100 g spinach
10 ginkgo nuts
5 tablespoons pine nuts
6 cups water
Fine salt to taste

1. Wash and rinse the white rice. Soak in water for about 1 hour.
2. In a pot, bring water to a boil and add ginkgo nuts. Cook for 3 minutes and shock them in ice water. Peel the skin from the ginkgo nuts.
3. In a blender, add ginkgo nuts, pine nuts and 1 cup of water. Puree well. Set aside.
4. In a blender, add well-washed spinach and 2 cups of water. Puree well. Sieve through a fine strainer or fine cheesecloth to get the juices only. Set aside.
5. In a blender, add soaked rice and 1 cup of water. Grind well.
6. In a thick-bottomed heavy pot (or non-stick pot), add the ground rice and 2 cups of water. Over low heat, stir with a wooden spoon (or rubber spatula) until rice is fully cooked with a porridge-like consistency.
7. Add nut puree and spinach juices. Stir and cook until everything is blended well.
8. Season with salt and serve.

SPINACH is an effective remedy and cure for hematochezia (bloody stool) caused by constipation or hemorrhoids. Spinach also helps individuals with night vision loss and various skin related allergies. **GINKGO NUTS** are effective in remedying respiratory conditions like reducing cough and sputum, and asthma. Ginkgo nuts are also effective in child polyuria and adult incontinence. However, ginkgo nuts do contain a small amount of toxins, so they are better to be eaten cooked and within 10 kernels per day.

SOUPS & NOODLES

SOUPS

Serving soup is one of the unique characteristics of a Korean meal. Soup based food includes soups and stews called jjigae. Soups are cooked with 1 or 2 main ingredients and are served to each person individually. People often like to eat their rice by putting it in the soup. Stews are cooked with more ingredients and with less water. People often eat chunks of the ingredients first, and mix their rice with the stew soup afterwards. If you use vegetable stock (boiled water with dried shiitake mushrooms, Korean radish, and kelp) to cook soups or stews, it will enhance its savory taste. If you eat too much soup, it can disturb digestion, but soups are much welcomed, especially during the winter, to warm the body.

NOODLES

There is a saying in Korean temples: Noodles make monks smile. The glutens in wheat and beans are an excellent source of proteins for vegetarian monks. If you add the juices of vegetable leaves or root vegetables to the flour dough, it will not only make the noodles colorful and more tasteful, but can also aid in the digestion of the glutens in flour.

Saeng-baechu-doenjang-guk

KOREAN SOYBEAN PASTE SOUP WITH NAPA CABBAGE

sweet and savory together in perfect harmony

Napa cabbage is most commonly used to make kimchi, but it is also good for Korean pancakes, salads, and braised dishes. Cabbage is helpful in the digestion process and soybean paste can also aid in stimulating bowel movements. Soybean paste soup is one of the most popular dishes in Korean cuisine, along with kimchi stew.

Serves 4-6
Preparation time: 10 minutes
Cooking time: 30 minutes

600 g napa cabbage

2 tablespoons Korean soybean paste

1 Korean green chili pepper, seeded and minced

1 Korean red chili pepper, seeded and minced

6 cups vegetable stock

1. Wash the napa cabbage. Slice the leaves in halves lengthwise and cut into 2 cm wide bias strips. Strain well in a colander.
2. In a pot, add vegetable stock. Bring to a boil, then add Korean soybean paste. Stir well to loosen the paste.
3. Add the napa cabbage. Bring to a boil, then reduce the heat and let simmer for about 20 minutes.
4. Add minced chili peppers. Turn off the heat.
5. Ladle soup in a bowl and serve.

NAPA CABBAGE is an effective remedy for indigestion and stomach ulcers. It also promotes regularity in urination and bowel movements. It improves cardiovascular functions, and even helps recovery from hangovers. It can also lower the body temperature.

SOUP vs STEW
Soups have more liquid than solid ingredients, while stews have more chunks of ingredients than liquid. Stews are usually saltier than soups.

Nok-cha-sujebi

GREEN TEA SUJEBI SOUP (HAND-TORN NOODLE)

a refreshing broth imbued with a hint of green tea

Drinking green tea can lighten your body as it helps digest gluten in foods made of flour. The soothing color and the smooth, refreshing taste of green tea can ease the body and clear the mind.

Serves 4-6
Preparation time: 15 minutes
Cooking time: 20 minutes

20 g green tea powder

2 cups all-purpose flour

60 g dried shiitake mushrooms, soaked in water

100 g potato, sliced into 0.3 cm half moon shapes

100 g zucchini, sliced into 0.3 cm half moon shapes

1 tablespoon soy sauce

7 cups vegetable stock

1 cup water

Fine salt to taste

1. In a mixing bowl, add green tea powder and flour. Add 1 cup of water. Stir well.
2. When water is absorbed and mixture looks flaky, use your hand to form the dough into a ball.
3. Knead until dough is smooth and soft, about 10 minutes. Cover with damp towel and set aside.
4. Remove the stems from the shiitake mushrooms and julienne them.
5. In a pot, add the vegetable stock and bring to a boil.
6. Add soy sauce and shiitake mushrooms to the stock.
7. **MAKE SUJEBI:** Have a bowl of water ready. Hold the dough in one hand, wet the other hand and pull off a small amount of dough by pinching, then flatten them into shape. Tear them directly into the boiling soup.
8. Bring sujebi and stock to a boil, then add potato and zucchini. Bring the soup back to a boil.
9. Season with fine salt and serve.

GREEN TEA can help fight cancer and suppress inflammation. It can help balance blood sugar levels, fight vascular diseases, and are high in antioxidants that have anti-aging properties.

Namul-bibim-myeon

COLD NOODLES
WITH ASSORTED VEGETABLES

an appetizing potpourri of spicy goodness

Seasonal vegetables are the best ingredients to use with mixed noodles. If you use the organic vegetables harvested from your own garden, you can create a variety of beautiful flavors. Fresh vegetables seasoned with red chili paste seasoning paired with cold noodles will certainly stimulate the appetite.

———————

ALL EDIBLE VEGETABLES are referred to as namul in Korean. Cold Noodles with Assorted Vegetables can be made with any edible vegetables grown in a garden or in an unpolluted natural environment to highlight an assortment of textures and flavors. **THE ASTER SABER** helps to warm up the body, promotes blood circulation, and eases body aches. **SPRING PARSLEY**, rich in beta-carotene, helps to suppress the growth of cancerous cells and promotes healthy vision. It also is an effective remedy for allergies. **SHEPHERD'S PURSE**, rich in a variety of vitamins, aids recovery from fatigue, is effective in alleviating hemorrhages, and promotes healthy liver function to benefit body detoxification.

Serves 3-4
Preparation time: 10 minutes
Cooking time: 7 minutes

140 g Korean medium-thick wheat noodles
100 g aster saber
100 g spring parsley
100 g shepherd's purse
Coarse sea salt to taste, for blanching vegetables and boiling Korean medium-thick wheat noodles

SEASONED KOREAN RED CHILI PASTE SAUCE:
MIX ALL INGREDIENTS
2 tablespoons Korean red chili paste
3 tablespoons Korean fermented green plum extract
2 tablespoons perilla seed oil
1 tablespoon grounded sesame seeds
1 teaspoon Korean red chili powder, fine

VARIATIONS:
The vegetables can be substituted with cabbage, cucumber, lettuce, or any fresh seasonal greens.

1. Add salt to boiling water, blanch all vegetables separately. Shock them in ice water. Drain and squeeze water out, and set aside.
2. Boil noodles in well salted water. Rinse the starch off in cold water. Drain well.
3. In a mixing bowl, add noodles and seasoned red chili paste sauce. Toss well to mix.
4. Add all vegetables and toss to mix.
5. Plate and serve.

SALADS

SALADS

Salads are uncooked, raw foods with minimal use of seasonings; the vegetables come together to create a harmonious dish. Saengjeori (raw fresh mixed salad) is made of fresh sprouts or other soft raw vegetables combined with a dressing. Muchim is a dish of lightly boiled vegetables in sea salt water, rinsed in cold water, then mixed with soybean paste, soy sauce, or red chili paste. The freshness of salads will last longer if served in a ceramic bowl that had been baked in a kiln over 1400°C heat.

Icheon, where I live, is also famous for its ceramics. If food is served in good earthenware, the freshness and taste will last longer. Ceramics made in a kiln that reaches temperatures over 1400°C are the best to use.

Doenjang-yangnyeom-chaeso-muchim

SALAD WITH KOREAN SOYBEAN PASTE DRESSING

an eclectic mix of lush vegetables complemented by fermentation enzymes

---

Serves 3-4
Preparation time: 15 minutes
Cooking time: 3 minutes

100 g iceberg lettuce

70 g perilla leaves

70 g angelica leaves (may substitute with celery leaves)

70 g chicory

50 g red cabbage

KOREAN SOYBEAN PASTE DRESSING:

1 tablespoon Korean soybean paste

2 tablespoons persimmon vinegar

2 tablespoons fermented magnolia berry extract

3 tablespoons fermented green plum, purple shiso leaf extract

5 tablespoons perilla seed powder

1. Wash iceberg lettuce, perilla leaves, angelica leaves, and chicory. Cut into bite-sized pieces.
2. Cut the core out from the red cabbage and fine julienne.
3. Make dressing by blending Korean soybean paste, vinegar, and both extracts in a blender.
4. Transfer the mixture to a mixing bowl, add perilla seed powder and combine well.
5. In a mixing bowl, toss the vegetables with the dressing.
6. Plate and serve.

Seasoned with soybean paste dressing, this salad of various seasonal leafy vegetables, root vegetables, or fruit offer quite the refreshing flavors.

KOREAN SOYBEAN PASTE, doenjang, is a traditional Korean sauce that allows the body to help better absorb the nutrients of soybeans; the rate of absorption fairly is low at its natural state. This fermented sauce can help maintain a balanced diet in nutrients for those individuals whose diet primarily consists of rice and wheat, by providing high levels of protein and key amino acids. Other benefits include detoxification of the body by aiding in liver functions.

Sagwa-mallaengi-muchim

REHYDRATED APPLE SALAD

bright and crispy with plenty of flavor

Dried apple or other seasonal dried fruits are not only great as snacks or appetizers on their own, but can be used as delicious ingredients.

Serves 3-4
Preparation time: 5 minutes
Cooking time: 3 minutes

---

80 g dried apples
1 Korean green chili pepper
1 tablespoon perilla seed oil
1 tablespoon roasted sesame seeds

SEASONED SAUCE: MIX ALL INGREDIENTS
1 tablespoon Korean red chili paste
1 tablespoon fermented green plum extract
1 teaspoon soy sauce
1 teaspoon Korean red chili powder
1 teaspoon ginger juice

1. Rinse dried apples in running water and hydrate them lightly.
2. Remove the seeds and pith from chili and fine julienne.
3. In a mixing bowl, add seasoned sauce and rehydrated apples. Mix well.
4. Add fine julienned chili and perilla seed oil. Toss together.
5. Sprinkle sesame seeds and serve.

DRIED APPLES are delightfully chewy and packed with natural sugars, making it ideal as a children's snack. Apples soothe the stomach, ease thirst, help digestion and can control diarrhea. It is plentiful in dietary fibers that prevent constipation, and the pectin in apples lowers cholesterol while also helping to control hypertension and hyperlipidemia.

SIMPLIFIED WAY TO DEHYDRATE FRUIT
Slice the fruit into 0.3~0.7 cm slices depending on the water content of the fruit. Spread out the sliced fruit in a bamboo basket or large tray and dry under sunlight. If weather does not permit, use a food dehydrator or bake the sliced fruit in a pan over low heat. It is best to keep dried fruit in an airtight container or vacuumed pack with a desiccant, and stored in a cool location or refrigerator.

KIMCHI & PICKLES

KIMCHI

When vegetables are salted, the distinct smell of fresh vegetables are removed and they can be prepared to be preserved for a longer period of time. During the fermentation and preservation process, the beneficial bacteria in the vegetables will actively multiply. Together with the natural microbes in our body, these beneficial bacteria strengthen our immune system and promote healthy digestion.

In general, there are two kinds of kimchi. Regular kimchi is made with red chili powder while white kimchi, fermented in salt water, does not use red chili powder.

PICKLES

All kinds of vegetables, from leaves, roots, even flowers or fruits, can be used for pickles with soy sauce, soybean paste, red chili paste, salt, vinegar, organic sugar, or fermented extracts. You can use raw or lightly boiled vegetables, but it is important not to let the vegetables turn soggy when making pickles; to retain crunchiness, it is best to pour boiled salt water directly onto the vegetables to blanch them. Afterwards, press the vegetables with heavy stones so the seasoning can permeate fully into the vegetables. Pickles can be kept in a cool area or in the refrigerator.

Oi-baek-kimchi

CUCUMBER WHITE KIMCHI

a burst of coolness and refreshment in one bite

Cucumbers can be used to make kimchi, pickles, or salads and can even be used braised or fried. Since it is a very light dish, cucumber white kimchi can be consumed immediately, but fermented cucumber white kimchi tastes even more tangy and refreshing.

Serves 4-8
Preparation time: 40 minutes
Cooking time: 5 minutes

5 cucumbers

200 g Korean daikon radish, fine julienne

2 cups Korean pear, juiced

2 cups water (drinking water)

3 tablespoons ginger juice

1/2 cup coarse salt

1 tablespoon fine salt

1. Wash cucumbers and cut into 5 cm long pieces.
2. Slit the cucumbers in quarters with one end still intact. Do not cut all the way through.
3. In a pot, add 3 cups of water and 1/2 cup of coarse salt. Bring to a boil.
4. Blanch the cucumbers by pouring hot salted water over them. Let them rest for 30 minutes.
5. Drain the salted water and rinse the cucumbers.
6. In a mixing bowl, add radish and fine salt. Mix well.
7. Stuff the radish julienne into the slits in the cucumbers.
8. In a mixing bowl, add pear juice, ginger juice and 2 cups of drinking water. Mix well.
9. In a separate container, arrange the stuffed cucumbers neatly and pour the juice mixture over.
10. Cover and rest in room temperature for about 1 day, then store in the refrigerator.

* Kimchi can be served fresh or aged.
* 2-3 days of fermentation is preferred. This will build up the umami flavors.

CUCUMBERS are high in water content and help to lower body temperatures and quench thirst, especially during the summer. It is low in calories and has diuretic effects to ease puffiness and swelling, and is helpful for those trying to control weight.

BELL PEPPERS are low in calories, rich in dietary fibers, and has a high water content that eases constipation and helps control weight gain. It contains high levels of vitamin C and lycopene which boosts the immune system and has anti-aging properties. The pyrazine in yellow paprika helps to prevents blood circulation diseases, specifically blood coagulation disorders.

Norang-paprika-baek-kimchi

WHITE NAPA CABBAGE KIMCHI WITH YELLOW BELL PEPPER

fresh and crunchy with a vibrant yellow hue

I created this kimchi recipe to introduce the flavors of Korean kimchi to the world, so anyone can enjoy the distinct taste of kimchi. Yellow bell peppers are easily found everywhere, and its bright yellow colors make this kimchi even more appetizing. It is refreshing and crunchy and requires only two to three days of fermentation.

Serves 4-8
Preparation time:
1 hour 10 minutes
Cooking time: 5 minutes

800 g hearts of napa cabbages
1/3 cup barley
300 g yellow bell pepper, seeded
300 g Korean pear, peeled and cored
20 g ginger, peeled
1 tablespoon fine salt
1 cup coarse salt (about 1/2 cup for cabbages, and another 1/2 cup for the brine)
4 cups water (cold water in the summer and lukewarm water in the winter)

1. Cut the napa cabbages in halves. Salt the cabbages by sprinkling coarse salt between the leaves. Make the brine mixture. Place the napa cabbages in brine for roughly 1 hour.

2. In a pot, add 3 cups of water and 1/3 cups of barley. * Bring to a boil and simmer for 20 minutes. After the barley is cooked, drain, and reserve 1 1/2 cups of the boiled barley water.

3. In a blender, add Korean pear and ginger. Blend and strain through a fine strainer or fine cheesecloth. Save the juice (about 1 1/2 cups).

4. In a blender, add the yellow bell pepper. Blend and strain through fine strainer or fine cheesecloth. Save the juice (about 1 1/2 cups).

* Cooked rice can be used in place of **cooked barley**.

5. In a mixing bowl, add barley water, pear and ginger juice, yellow bell pepper juice, and fine salt. Mix together well.

6. Rinse the napa cabbages and arrange them in a container. Pour the juice mixture over the cabbages.

7. Cover and let rest in room temperature for about 1 to 2 days, then store in the refrigerator.

Modeum-chaeso-jeorim

ASSORTED PICKLED VEGETABLES

sweet and tart with peppery overtones

With the purple hue from the red cabbage and unique aroma from the celery, this pickled dish offers a dynamic combination of flavors. It can be made anywhere in the world by using any kinds of vegetables found locally.

Serves 4-8
Preparation time: 25 minutes
Cooking time: 3 minutes

400 g Korean daikon radish
2 cucumbers
2 stalks of celery
5 leaves of red cabbage
1 Korean green chili pepper
1 Korean red chili pepper
5 tablespoons vinegar
3 tablespoons organic sugar
1 tablespoon fine salt
3 cups water

1. Cut radish, cucumbers, and red cabbage into pieces roughly the size of a pinky finger (1 cm x 4 cm).
2. Remove the tough fibers from the celery and cut into same size as other vegetables.
3. Slice chili peppers about into pieces 0.5 cm long. Remove the seeds.
4. In a pot, add 3 cups of water and bring to a boil. Add sugar and salt, bring back to a boil. Add vinegar, then turn off the heat.
5. In a container, arrange the vegetables in order of radish, cucumbers, celery, red cabbage, and chilis. Pour the hot pickling liquid over the vegetables.
6. Rest in room temperature for about 6 hours then cover and store in the refrigerator.

KOREAN RADISH helps digestive functions, protects stomach walls, and prevents the common cold. Celery, with its distinctive aroma, lowers body temperatures, promotes discharge of bodily wastes through urination, and is also good for treating symptoms of insomnia. Red cabbage helps to prevent aging through the disposal of free oxygen radicals, protects vision health, and alleviates eye fatigue.

Hansang-charim

ONE TRAY SERVING

Each was good enough for a meal,
but together they became a well balanced whole.

Korean Buddhist monks follow the "3 dishes in 1 meal" rule; rice, soup and one side dish are enough for a complete, balanced meal. Balwoo is the term for the bowls used by Buddhist monks and nuns. Literally, balwoo means, "a bowl that holds exactly as much as needed," no more, no less.
Bowls of four slightly different sizes are stacked together as one. Each are used for rice, soup, a side dish, and water. Leftover drinking water is used to clean other bowls after a meal.

I designed this book so that each section illustrates a single, complete "one tray serving."

PART 1
Sticky Rice Wrapped in Lotus Leaf
Korean Soybean Paste Soup with Napa Cabbage
Rehydrated Apple Salad

PART 2.

WOOKWAN'S
TASTE OF SHARING

from a sincere heart

STIR-FRIED

STIR-FRIED

Stir-frying is a way of cooking food in a pan with cooking oil over high heat. When stir-frying vegetables, it is best to use cooking oil that has a high smoke point such as grapeseed oil, sunflower seed oil, or pure olive oil. When making seasoned raw vegetable dishes or salads, it is preferable to use low smoke point oils like sesame oil, perilla seed oil, and extra virgin olive oil. To best maintain the natural flavors and aromas, fry vegetables rapidly with a small amount of oil and add the seasonings quickly.

Danhobak-broccoli-bokkeum

STIR-FRIED KABOCHA SQUASH AND BROCCOLI

a synergy of colors that augments flavors

When you cook this dish, stir-fry the kabocha squash first, being careful not to break apart its shape. Stir occasionally over medium heat to season evenly. Roasted kabocha squash seeds can also be used for cooking.

Serves 3-4
Preparation time: 10 minutes
Cooking time: 5 minutes

300 g kabocha squash, peeled and seeded
200 g broccoli, with stems cut off
2 tablespoons perilla seed oil
1 tablespoon coarse salt
1 tablespoon black sesame seeds

SEASONED SOY SAUCE:
MIX ALL INGREDIENTS
2 tablespoons soy sauce
2 tablespoons rice syrup
1 tablespoon fermented green plum extract

* USE OF KABOCHA SQUASH SEEDS: Wash the seeds and dry thoroughly in a tray. After they are fully dried, cut off the end of each seed and peel off the skins. They are now good to be stored and can be used to fry with other dishes.

1. Cut kabocha squash into large dices, about 2 cm x 2 cm.
2. Cut broccoli to a similar size as the kabocha squash dices.
3. Add coarse salt in boiling water. Blanch kabocha squash for 2 minutes then shock in ice water.
4. Add salt to boiling water, blanch broccoli in the water from step 3 for 1 minute, then shock in ice water.
5. Heat the pan, add perilla seed oil and begin stir-frying the kabocha squash.
6. Add the seasoned soy sauce and stir carefully.
7. Add the broccoli and stir. Make sure the vegetables soak up the seasoned soy sauce for a nice, even glaze.
8. Garnish with black sesame seeds and serve.

KABOCHA SQUASH is good for reducing puffiness and swelling of the body, especially for women. It helps individuals with weight problems, high levels of cholesterol, and diabetes. Broccoli belongs to the mustard family of vegetables and are rich in vitamin C as well as calcium and potassium. It can help control gastrointestinal disorders.

Ueong-bokkeum

STIR-FRIED BURDOCK ROOT

enjoy the sweet and earthy flavors of burdock root, loaded with fiber

Julienned burdock roots make it easy to season and using thin pieces enhance their crunchy texture. This dish produces a harmonized flavor alongside the green peppers and carrots. Use a burdock root that is straight and even in thickness.

Serves 3-4
Preparation time: 15 minutes
Cooking time: 7 minutes

300 g burdock roots, peeled and fine julienned (about 5 cm long)

* **TIP:** peel using back of the knife

5 Korean green chili peppers, seeded and fine julienned (about 5 cm long)

150 g carrots, fine julienned (about 5 cm long)

2 tablespoons soy sauce

2 tablespoons grapeseed oil

2 tablespoons rice syrup

1 tablespoon fermented green plum extract

1 tablespoon roasted sesame seeds, ground

1 tablespoon perilla seed oil

1. Heat the pan, add grapeseed oil and start stir-frying the burdock roots.
2. When burdock roots are par-cooked, add carrots and continue to stir-fry.
3. Add soy sauce, rice syrup, and Korean fermented green plum extract. Stir-fry evenly until burdock roots and carrots soak up the flavors.
4. Stir in green chili peppers. Turn off heat, add perilla seed oil and ground sesame seeds, and stir well.
5. Plate and serve.

THE BURDOCK ROOT has plenty of dietary fibers and oligosaccharides that supports healthy bowel movements and prevents constipation. It also contains a high level of natural insulin called inulin, which balances blood sugar levels in the body.

Hodu-mareun-jepiip-bokkeum

STIR-FRIED WALNUTS WITH DRIED PRICKLY-ASH PEPPER LEAVES (SICHUAN PEPPER)

nuts with an added zing to liven the senses

The flavors of the perilla seed oil and rice syrup reduces and balances the bitterness of the walnut's inner skin which is so abundant in nutrients. Other pungent vegetables like celery, parsley, or cilantro can be used to replace the prickly-ash pepper leaves. These vegetables can be used either raw or dried.

Serves 3-4
Preparation time: 7 minutes
Cooking time: 5 minutes

300 g walnuts, washed and dried

10 g dried prickly-ash pepper leaves, with stems cut off

1 tablespoon perilla seed oil

1 tablespoon grapeseed oil

1 tablespoon rice syrup

1 tablespoon roasted sesame seeds

1 teaspoon fine salt

VARIATIONS: Dried parsley leaves, celery leaves, or cilantro leaves can be used in place of the prickly-ash pepper leaves.

1. Heat the pan, add grapeseed oil and walnuts. Stir-fry well and add salt.
2. Add in the rice syrup and stir.
3. Add prickly-ash pepper leaves and stir. Turn off the heat and add perilla seed oil and sesame seeds. Stir well to mix.
4. Plate and serve.

WALNUTS are beneficial in alleviating asthmatic conditions and other lung related diseases. **PRICKLY-ASH PEPPER LEAVES** have insecticidal effects against intestinal roundworms and also controls harmful intestinal bacteria. Prickly-ash pepper leaves further aid digestive functions, soothes symptoms of colic (which is common after eating cold foods), and is also effective for treating diarrhea.

BRAISED & STEAMED

BRAISED & STEAMED

Steaming is a healthy moist-heat cooking method. Before steaming, it is important to cut the ingredients into proper sizes depending on their firmness and density. Steam food over a high heat first, then lower to a medium heat after the water boils. Similar to steaming, braising is another cooking method using steam and moisture extracted from seasoned foods. When seasoned food is about to boil or after it is properly seared, turn the heat to low to avoid burning.

Gaji-yangnyeom-jjim

BRAISED EGGPLANT WITH SEASONED SOY SAUCE

simply light and tender, with a sumptuous flair

Use long, dark purple, glossy, and juicy eggplants for this dish. Soft eggplants and the green zucchini with a small touch of seasoning truly heightens their natural flavors. Since the dish does not use any cooking oil, it is easy on the digestive system and is especially good for patients and children.

───────

EGGPLANTS contain high levels of dietary fiber, and so are helpful in preventing constipation and effective for weight control. They are also beneficial for maintaining eye health, can relieve inflammation, and help fatigue recovery. **ZUCCHINI** is low in calories, and also high in nutrients and dietary fibers. They promote vascular health, protect the stomach, and aid in digestive and nutrient absorption functions.

Serves 3-4
Preparation time: 15 minutes
Cooking time: 7 minutes

3 Asian eggplants

100 g zucchini, fine julienned (about 3 cm long)

SEASONED SOY SAUCE: MIX ALL INGREDIENTS

2 tablespoons soy sauce

3 tablespoons rice syrup

1/2 cup vegetable stock

1. Cut the eggplants into halves, lengthwise. Cut into approximately 5 cm long pieces.
2. Score the skin side, keeping roughly 1 cm between each line.
3. Stuff zucchini into the slits on the eggplants.
4. In a pot, arrange the stuffed eggplants and pour the seasoned soy sauce over them.
5. Steam over medium heat for about 7 minutes.
6. Plate and serve.

Yeongeun-hodu-doenjang-jjim

STEAMED LOTUS ROOT AND WALNUT WITH KOREAN SOYBEAN PASTE

a banquet of tastes and textures

The unique texture of the lotus roots and walnuts balance harmoniously with the flavors of the soybean paste and spicy peppers. This recipe may require several trials to find the golden ratio of the soybean paste to peppers because taste of the soybean paste may vary and the spiciness of each pepper different. However, it is a great dish to practice the study of flavors, remembering taste of each ingredient in your head.

Serves 3-4
Preparation time: 15 minutes
Cooking time: 10 minutes

400 g lotus roots, peeled and sliced into 1 cm thick pieces

100 g walnuts, roughly chopped

1 Korean green chili pepper, brunoise (finely diced)

1 Korean red chili pepper, brunoise (finely diced)

SEASONED KOREAN SOYBEAN PASTE SAUCE:
MIX ALL INGREDIENTS

1 tablespoon Korean soybean paste

2 tablespoons fermented green plum extract

1 tablespoon perilla seed oil

1 teaspoon ginger, minced

1. Mix seasoned Korean soybean paste sauce with the walnuts and chili peppers.
2. Carve the slices in a scalloped pattern around the holes of the lotus roots to make a flower shapes.
3. Top lotus root slices with the walnut mixture.
4. After boiling water, place lotus root slices in the steamer. Steam for about 10 minutes.
5. Plate and serve.

LOTUS ROOTS stimulate the appetite, aid in digestion, and can control diarrhea. It helps alleviate gastrointestinal diseases and can also improve the conditions of anemia and dizziness. In addition, lotus roots have hemostatic properties, and can even reduce coughing and phlegm production.

GRILLED DISHES
& PANCAKES

GRILLED DISHES

There are two ways to grill: grill the ingredients after seasoning them, or grill the ingredients first then brush on seasoning, and then grill again. If you use a pan to grill, you need to use cooking oil and control the heat carefully as to not burn the seasoning. Charcoal grilling leaves the aroma of charcoal on the food itself and makes the dish even more flavorful. You can present various raw vegetables along with seasoned grilled dishes to enhance both taste and nutritional value, and satisfy all five senses.

PANCAKES

Rice cakes are made of steamed or boiled grain flours. Jangtteok (Korean pancake with red chili paste) is a type of fried rice cake dish seasoned with soybean paste or red chili paste. Jeon is the term for a variety of types of "Korean pancakes." They can be made with fried vegetables or other ingredients coated with batter of sticky rice flour or whole purpose flour.

Saesongi-beoseot-gui

GRILLED KING OYSTER MUSHROOMS

bask in the clean and intense flavor of mushrooms

Good king oyster mushrooms have a strong scent and firm yet elastic stalks. You can either grill raw king oyster mushrooms over charcoal or seasoned with soy sauce and served with pine nuts. When you serve oyster mushrooms to guests, it is better to cut them into bite sized pieces.

Serves 4-5
Preparation time: 13 minutes
Cooking time: 7 minutes

5 king oyster mushrooms
1 Korean green chili pepper, seeded and finely minced
1 tablespoon of pine nuts, finely minced
Coarse salt to taste

SEASONED SOY SAUCE: MIX ALL INGREDIENTS
2 tablespoons soy sauce
2 tablespoons perilla seed oil
1 tablespoon rice syrup
1 tablespoon fermented green plum extract

1. Cut the king oyster mushrooms in halves, lengthwise.
2. Score the outside (not the cut side). Leave about 1 cm between the cuts.
3. Add salt to boiling water, blanch the mushrooms and shock in ice water. Drain and dry well.
4. Grill the mushrooms in a griddle (or non-stick pan) without any oil until the mushrooms have some color.
5. Add the seasoned soy sauce little by little to the mushrooms and continue to grill until mushrooms are well seasoned.
6. Sprinkle minced chili and pine nuts on top.
7. Plate and serve.

KING OYSTER MUSHROOMS have anticancerous properties and can enhance liver functions and overall digestion. It is also abundant in dietary fiber making it effective for those on a diet. Large oyster mushrooms can also alleviate constipation, lessen symptoms of hypertension, and help the prevention of osteoporosis. Abundant in vitamin C and E, mushrooms are also effective for skin care.

Cheonggochu-jangtteok

KOREAN GREEN CHILI PEPPER PANCAKE WITH RED CHILI PASTE

a zest that revives the palate

This pancake, especially when accompanied by rice balls, is sufficient enough to be a meal on its own. We tend to cook less salty foods nowadays, but in old times when food was more scarce, a bowl of rice with a very salty pancake often made up a single meal.

Serves 3-4
Preparation time: 10 minutes
Cooking time: 10 minutes

8 Korean green chili peppers, seeded and minced
2 Korean red chili peppers, seeded and minced
100 g tofu (firm), crushed and drained
1/2 cup all-purpose flour
1 tablespoon Korean red chili paste
1 1/2 teaspoons Korean soybean paste
1 tablespoon vegetable stock
3 tablespoons grapeseed oil

1. In a mixing bowl, add all-purpose flour, vegetable stock, tofu, chili peppers, Korean red chili paste, and Korean soybean paste. Mix well to make a light dough. Let the dough rest for a few minutes.
   * Watch the moisture content from the tofu and sauces. At first, the dough will look a bit hard or dry, but after letting it rest, you will notice that it becomes a bit looser by the moisture from the tofu and sauces.
2. Heat the griddle (or non-stick pan) and add the grapeseed oil.
3. Shape a spoonful of dough and add to pan, then gently flatten to make it into a disk shape.
4. Griddle both sides of pancake.
5. Plate and serve.

Rich in vitamin C, the **CHILI PEPPER** alleviates joint and nerve pains, and has anticancer benefits as well. Capsaicin, the component of the pepper that produces the spicy, burning sensation, aids those on a diet and reduces stress; however, it can be harmful to the stomach if too much is consumed.

Samsaeg-yeongeun-jeon

TRI-COLOR LOTUS ROOT PANCAKE

a medley of colors that catches the eye

You can dye lotus roots with various colorful foods such as green tea powder, gardenia powder, or prickly pear cactus powder. Each powder not only has a beautiful color, but also medicinal benefits for the body. It's important for the food preparer to know the medicinal benefits of each ingredient while cooking.

Serves 3-4
Preparation time: 25 minutes
Cooking time: 10 minutes

400 g lotus roots

5 g green tea powder

5 g gardenia powder

5 g prickly pear cactus powder

1 cup all-purpose flour, divided into 3 portions

3 tablespoons grapeseed oil

1 teaspoon fine salt

120 ml water, divided into 3 portions

VARIATIONS: You can substitute gardenia powder with turmeric powder, and cactus pear powder with red beet powder.

1. Peel the lotus roots, and slice into pieces roughly 0.5 cm thick.
2. Carve the slices in a scalloped pattern around the holes of the lotus roots to make a flower shapes.
3. Add salt to boiling water, blanch the lotus roots, and set aside. (No shocking needed)
4. Make a green batter by mixing green tea powder, 1/3 cup of flour and 40 ml of water.
5. Make a yellow batter by mixing gardenia powder, 1/3 cup of flour and 40 ml of water.
6. Make a red batter by mixing pear cactus powder, 1/3 cup of flour and 40 ml of water.
7. Heat a griddle (or non-stick pan) and add some grapeseed oil.
8. Batter lotus root slices with the three different batters separately, and pan-fry both sides until golden brown.
9. Plate and serve.

GARDENIA POWDER is made of dried and finely ground red-ripe gardenia fruits, and is used as a natural ingredient for yellow food coloring. It reduces body temperatures and helps to purify blood. Gardenia powder is effective for controlling skin related disorders and can also soothe nerves, alleviate insomnia, and reduce pains.
PRICKLY PEAR CACTUS POWDER is made from the fruits of the prickly pear cactus. When ripened, it is dark red in color; it is then harvested, dried, finely ground, and used as a natural ingredient for red food coloring. It promotes bone health, and is effective for individuals with asthma. When taken over time, the prickly pear cactus can boost the immune system.

SNACKS & JELLY

SNACKS

Bugak is a traditional Korean snack made of fried vegetables or seaweed that is coated with sticky rice flour. Since it can becomes soggy with moisture when stored, and the cooking oil can become oxidized by the sunlight, it is better to keep bugak in an airtight container or to cook just enough to eat and serve at one sitting.

JELLY

Korean jelly, called yanggaeng, is a Korean dessert or snack that has a texture similar to soft jelly. It is made of agar, a gelatinous substance obtained from various kinds of red seaweed, instead of gelatin. Coffee beans, green tea powder, or extracts from various ingredients can be added for unique flavors, colors, and aromas to yanggaeng.

Gyeongwa-hyoso-gangjeong

MIXED FRUIT AND NUT BAR WITH FERMENTED MAGNOLIA BERRY EXTRACT

a great source of energy packed with nutrients

This snack was designed to satisfy the taste buds and to nourish the body. You can make enough to serve as a snack or dessert, but it has enough nutritional value to replace a meal.

Serves 4-8
Preparation time: 5 minutes
Cooking time: 30 minutes

60 g almonds, washed and dried

60 g cashew nuts, washed and dried

60 g walnuts, washed and dried

60 g macadamia nuts, washed and dried

60 g pine nuts

60 g dried cranberries

3 tablespoons roasted sesame seeds

5 tablespoons rice syrup

2 tablespoons maple syrup

3 tablespoons fermented magnolia berry extract

3 tablespoons grapeseed oil

1. Heat the pan and add grapeseed oil.
2. Add almonds, cashew nuts, walnuts and macadamia nuts. Stir-fry until par-cooked.
3. When nuts are par-cooked, add pine nuts and continue to stir-fry. Set aside.
4. In a separate pan, add the rice syrup and maple syrup and bring to a boil over low heat. Turn off heat.
5. Add nut mixture to the syrup and mix well first, then add in the dried cranberries and fermented magnolia berry extract to the mixture.
6. Transfer mixture to an oiled container and flatten.
7. Sprinkle sesame seeds on top. Let is slightly cool down before handling.
8. Cut to desired sizes and shapes. Plate and serve.

NUTS are rich in unsaturated fats and plentiful in linolenic acid and vitamin E. Nuts promote brain health, and can prevent arteriosclerosis, a vascular disease. Nuts consumed in small amounts on a daily basis is highly beneficial to the body, but excess consumption can cause weight gain due to their high caloric content.

Dasima-chal-bap-bugak

KELP CRISPS WITH STICKY RICE

a snowy rice flower blossom on a bed of kelp

This type of snack is called bugak in Korean, and is usually a fried dish. To make bugak, a sticky rice paste is used to coat various vegetables. When they are dry, they are then fried. Leaf vegetables, root vegetables, fruits, and seaweeds can be used for the recipe. For this bugak, use kelp that is thick and dark in color. If you want to store them for a longer period of time, be sure to keep well-dried kelp in an airtight container.

Serves 4-8
Preparation time: 8 hours
Cooking time: 10 minutes

200g dried kelp, thicker parts of the kelp
1 cup sticky rice, soaked in water for 1 hour
1/2 teaspoon fine salt
3 cups grapeseed oil

1. Cook the sticky rice to an al dente texture.
2. Wipe the kelp pieces with a damp towel and cut into pieces roughly 5 cm x 5 cm.
3. Place about a teaspoon of cooked sticky rice to the center of each piece of kelp.
4. Place them in a rack and dry until they are nicely hardened.
5. In a pot, add grapeseed oil and heat to about 180°C (350°F).
6. Fry them rice side first and flip to finish.
7. Plate and serve.

The algin (alginic acid) in **KELP** stimulates the effective release of intestinal waste, which can aid in preventing constipation and intestinal cancers. Kelp lowers cholesterol levels and stabilizes blood pressure. It can also prevent hair loss.

Coffee-yanggaeng

COFFEE JELLY

the deep aroma of coffee refreshes the palate

I came up with this snack while I was contemplating how to enjoy coffee in a more convenient way. One piece of jelly contains roughly one shot of espresso. You will be able to feel and enjoy the strong taste and aromas of the fresh coffee beans. One or two cups of coffee a day can be beneficial since the caffeine stimulates the body and mind.

Serves 4-8
Preparation time: 15 minutes
Cooking time: 30 minutes

200 ml coffee, brewed
100 ml rice syrup
100 ml water

10 g agar-agar powder
10 g organic sugar

1. Bloom agar-agar by combining the powder with 100 ml of water and letting rest for 5 minutes in room temperature.
2. Heat the bloomed agar-agar mixture in low-medium heat in a pot. Stir well until air bubbles appear (almost to its boiling point).
3. Add the brewed coffee and sugar to the mixture. Stir well until air bubbles appear (almost to its boiling point).
4. Add rice syrup, stir, and bring to a boil.
5. Turn off the heat. Pour the mixture into the molds and cool to harden.
6. Take them out and serve.

CAFFEINE in coffee stimulates blood circulation, helping to prevent cardiovascular diseases. It is also a diuretic and can aid in eliminating unpleasant breath. Coffee prevents drowsiness and stimulates brain activity to energize the body, but when taken during evening hours, coffee may obstruct sleep.

Nokcha-yanggaeng

GREEN TEA JELLY

the delicate essence of green tea cleanses the palate

The deep flavor and scent of the green tea refreshes the palate and dissolves any feeling of greasiness in the mouth after a meal.

Serves 4-8
Preparation time: 15 minutes
Cooking time: 30 minutes

30 g Korean green tea powder
100 ml rice syrup
300 ml water

10 g agar-agar powder
10 g organic sugar

1. In a bowl, add green tea powder and 300 ml of water. Mix well to make tea and set aside.
2. Bloom agar-agar by combining with 1/2 cup of water and letting rest for 5 minutes in room temperature.
3. Heat the bloomed agar-agar mixture in low-medium heat in a pot. Stir well until air bubbles appear (almost to its boiling point).
4. Add the green tea and sugar to the mixture. Stir well until air bubbles appear (almost to its boiling point).
5. Add rice syrup, stir, and bring to a boil.
6. Turn off the heat. Pour the mixture into the molds and cool to harden.
7. Take them out and serve.

AGAR-AGAR is made with seaweed from the red algae family. It is first sun-dried, boiled, then frozen. Agar-agar is low in calories yet is quite filling, making it an ideal food for those on a diet. Rich in dietary fiber, it alleviates constipation. It also has an effect on lowering blood pressure and reducing levels of bad cholesterol.

Hansang-charim

ONE TRAY SERVING

Each was good enough for a meal,
but together they became a well balanced whole.

PART 2
Stir-fried Burdock Root
Grilled King Oyster Mushrooms
Coffee Jelly and Green Tea Jelly

PART 3.

WOOKWAN'S
TASTE OF HARMONY

from coexistence of humans and nature

Cauliflower-juk

CAULIFLOWER PORRIDGE

nutrient rich with lively flavors that are nutty and slightly sweet

Cauliflower, with its mildly savory taste is an excellent ingredient for porridge, but can also be cooked with broccoli and added to a fried rice dish. The vegetable can also be pickled for a crunchy variation or even mashed like a potato for a healthy and hearty meal.

Serves 3-4
Preparation time: 4 hours
Cooking time: 30 minutes

1 cup short-grain brown rice
200 g cauliflower florets, small bite size
50 g broccoli florets, small bite size
Soy sauce to taste
Coarse salt to taste
7 cups vegetable stock

1. Wash and rinse the brown rice. Soak in water for about 4 hours.
2. Add salt to boiling water, blanch the cauliflower and broccoli, then shock in ice water and drain.
3. In a pot, boil brown rice in vegetable stock over medium heat.
4. When the rice starts to break down, add cauliflower and broccoli.
5. Continuously boil while stirring with a wooden spoon.
6. When all ingredients are cooked, season with soy sauce and serve.

CAULIFLOWER strengthens the heart and suppresses growth of cancerous cells. It is rich in minerals and vitamin C, and enhances activation of enzymes that detoxify body. It also aids in suppressing inflammation.

Dubu-avocado-salad

AVOCADO SALAD WITH TOFU

a soft, creamy, and tangy delight

Both avocado and tofu are ingredients rich in proteins and so this salad is an excellent protein supplement for vegetarians. The combination of soft avocado and tofu maximizes their flavors while lemon helps digestion.

Serves 3-4
Preparation time: 20 minutes
Cooking time: 7 minutes

3 avocados
120 g tofu, soft
15 g lemon rind
3 tablespoons extra virgin olive oil
2 tablespoons balsamic vinegar
1 tablespoon soy sauce

1. Blanch the tofu, rinse in cold water, then crush and drain well.
2. In a mixing bowl, add crushed tofu, soy sauce, and 1 tablespoon of olive oil. Mix well by hand.
3. Cut the avocados in half, take the pit out, and peel. Slice avocado thinly. Reserve the slices and trimmings separately.
4. Lay out the avocado slices and line them up neatly. Add some of the tofu mixture on top and wrap gently to make rolls.
5. In a mixing bowl, mix rest of tofu mixture and avocado trimmings together and make small balls with the mixture.
6. In a small serving bowl, add balsamic vinegar and 2 tablespoons of olive oil for a vinaigrette.
7. Arrange rolls and balls on a plate. Garnish with lemon peel and serve with the vinaigrette on side.

AVOCADOS have a wonderful variety of vitamins that our bodies need. They can reduces harmful cholesterol levels in the body and therefore prevent atherosclerosis. Its beta-carotene content protects the skin and prevents growth of cancerous cells. Avocados also have lutein which supports vision health and recovery from eye fatigue.

Gueun-konjac-broccoli rabe-muchim

BROCCOLI RABE SALAD WITH GRILLED KONJAC

a light and excellent meal alternative

Broccoli rabe, with its bitter yet somewhat sweet flavors, meets konjac for a uniquely delightful combination. The blanched and seasoned broccoli rabe and the grilled konjac slices with the spicy flavors of Korean red chili paste together come together in a filling and nourishing dish that can be eaten in place of rice. This dish is easy on the digestive system and does not weigh down the body.

Serves 3-4
Preparation time: 5 minutes
Cooking time: 10 minutes

300 g broccoli rabe
100 g konjac
1/2 teaspoon fine salt
1 tablespoon perilla seed oil
Olive oil for grilling
Coarse salt to taste

SEASONED KOREAN RED CHILI PASTE SAUCE:
MIX ALL INGREDIENTS

1 tablespoon Korean red chili paste
1 tablespoon fermented green plum extract
2 tablespoons vinegar
1 teaspoon roasted sesame seeds
1 teaspoon ginger juice

1. Wash broccoli rabe well.
2. Add salt to boiling water, blanch the broccoli rabe, and shock in ice water then squeeze the water out.
3. In mixing bowl, add broccoli rabe, 1/2 teaspoon of fine salt and 1 tablespoon of perilla seed oil. Toss well.
4. Slice the konjac into 3 cm x 5 cm slices. Score one side of the konjac slices.
5. Blanch konjac slices in boiling water, then shock in ice water and drain well.
6. Heat the pan, add olive oil, and grill konjac slices on both side until there is some color.
7. Tie the grilled konjac slices with the broccoli rabe. Arrange them on plate, drizzle with seasoned red chili paste sauce, and serve.

BROCCOLI RABE contains many vitamins and is full of minerals such as calcium, iron, and phosphorus, making it effective for preventing bone related diseases such as osteoporosis. **KONJAC** is made from the powdered form of its plant stem combined with calcium hydroxide. Rich in glucomannan, a dietary fiber, konjac provides the feeling of fullness when eaten, and so is helpful for those on a diet. It also aids in detoxifying the body and to prevent constipation.

Bangul-yangbaechu-nureungji-bokkeum

STIR-FRIED BRUSSELS SPROUTS WITH CRUNCHY RICE

a delectable fusion of crisp greens and nutty rice

Crunchy brussels sprouts and nutty rice make a delicious, healthy meal. Rich in many valuable nutrients, brussels sprouts can also be pickled with sweet and sour soy sauce and served as a tasty side dish.

Serves 3-4
Preparation time: 10 minutes
Cooking time: 10 minutes

200 g brussels sprouts, cut into halves

100 g cooked rice (short-grain)

2 tablespoons pomegranate seeds

20 g butter

2 tablespoons soy sauce

1 tablespoon ginger juice

Coarse salt to taste

1. Add salt to boiling water, blanch the brussels sprouts, and shock in ice water. Drain well.
2. Heat the pan and add 10 g of butter. Add one spoon of rice at a time to the pan and flatten to make small rice discs (like rice fonds). Pan-fry them until golden brown. Take the rice discs out and set aside.
3. Add 10 g of butter and brussels sprouts to the pan. Stir-fry over high heat, then season with soy sauce and ginger juice.
4. Add the rice discs and glaze them evenly.
5. Garnish with pomegranate seeds and serve.

BRUSSELS SPROUTS not only contain many vitamins, but are also rich in minerals that our body needs in minute quantities such as manganese, copper, potassium, phosphorus, and magnesium. It reduces inflammation, detoxifies the body, and helps to balance blood sugar levels. Brussels sprouts also protect the stomach and aid digestion.

Asparagus-yangsongi-beoseot-bokkeum

STIR-FRIED ASPARAGUS AND BUTTON MUSHROOMS

a flavor combination that wakes the taste buds

It is best to cook asparagus and button mushrooms with minimum amounts of seasoning in order to preserve their natural, subtle flavors. If you always cook with this mindset, you will truly begin to realize the importance of the quality of raw food materials. We need to be mindful of the fact that true flavors and aromas of food always come from the original ingredients, not from the seasonings.

Serves 3-4
Preparation time: 10 minutes
Cooking time: 5 minutes

———————

12 asparagus stalks
6 button mushrooms
10 g butter
1/2 teaspoon fine salt
Black pepper to taste
Coarse salt to taste

1. Trim and cut the asparagus in halves.
2. Cut the mushrooms in quarters.
3. Add salt in boiling water, blanch the asparagus, and shock in ice water. Drain well.
4. Heat the pan, add butter. Stir-fry asparagus first, then add the mushrooms and season with fine salt and black pepper.
5. Plate and serve.

———————

ASPARAGUS is a very healthy food ingredient with plenty of minerals and vitamins; it is particularly good for the prevention of gastrointestinal diseases. It contains rutin (also known as rutoside) which is thought to improve blood circulation and strengthen the cardiovascular system. It is also rich in vitamin K, proving effective for the prevention of osteoporosis. It is a balanced source of nutrition, especially for patients.

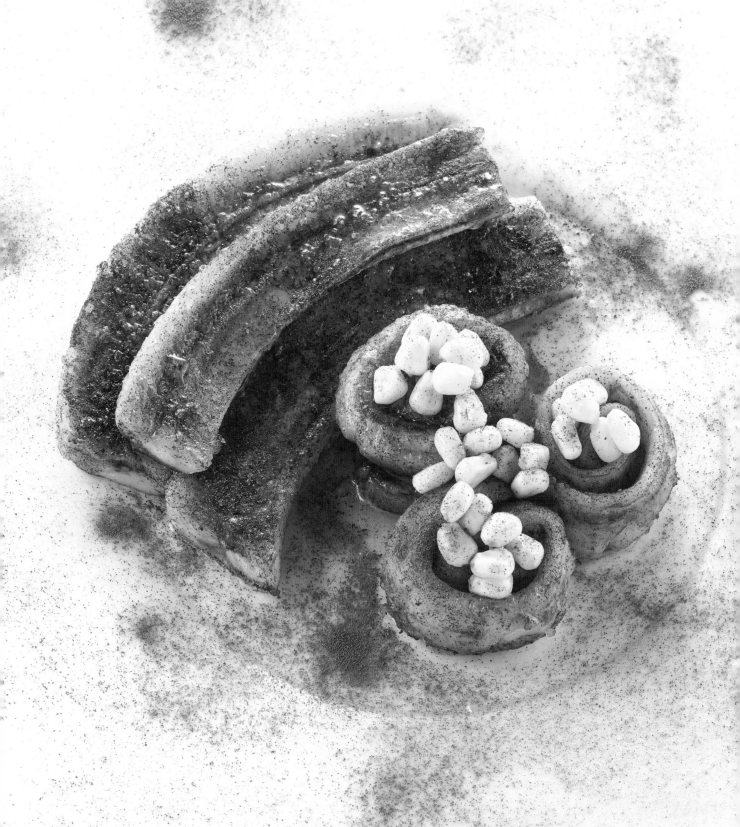

Norang-plantain-gui

GRILLED YELLOW PLANTAINS WITH STEAMED CORN (MADURO)

the perfect union of cinnamon and maple syrup

Plantains are delicious when fried like chips or french fries. Mashed plantains can also be used to enhance the flavors in a curry as it thickens it and makes it less salty and more nuanced. Well ripened plantains have a distinct scent similar to that of bananas and a sweet taste somewhat reminiscent of carrots.

Serves 3-4
Preparation time: 3 minutes
Cooking time: 7 minutes

4 yellow plantains

40 g corn kernels, steamed

2 tablespoons cinnamon powder

2 tablespoons maple syrup

1 tablespoon organic sugar

1 tablespoon coconut oil

Fine salt to taste

1. Peel plantains and trim each end. Slice the plantains lengthwise into 4 long pieces.
2. Heat the pan and add coconut oil. Pan-fry plantain slices on both sides until golden brown over medium heat.
3. Sprinkle salt and sugar on top.
4. Place plantain slices on the plate. Drizzle with maple syrup and sprinkle cinnamon powder.
5. Top with corn kernels and serve.

PLANTAINS are somewhat similar to bananas, but are lower in sugar and can be used at all stages of ripeness. When they are green, they can be used in stews, but when they are ripe and yellow, plantains can be used in desserts or as an ingredient for deep frying. With plenty of dietary fiber and carbohydrates, plantains are filling and healthy.

Beet-mu-jeon

BEET AND DAIKON RADISH PANCAKE

fall in love with the sweetness of root vegetables

Any dishes using beets will turn to a vibrant red in color. White radishes will turn the color of beets and their sweetness will be enhanced. Dried thin slices of beets can also be served fresh, as is, or fried as a snack.

Serves 3~4
Preparation time: 15 minutes
Cooking time: 10 minutes

300 g beets

100 g Korean daikon radishes

1 cup all-purpose flour

1 cup water

1 tablespoon fine salt

3 tablespoons grapeseed oil

1. Slice both beets and radishes into half-moon shapes, 0.5 cm thick.
2. In a pot, add 1 cup of water, salt, and the beet and radish slices. Boil for about 5 minutes. Drain and cool. Save the boiling water.
3. In a bowl, add the saved boiled water and flour to make a batter.
4. Add the beet and radish slices to the batter to coat.
5. Heat the pan and add grapeseed oil. Pan-fry the battered beet and radish slices until both sides are golden brown.
6. Plate and serve.

BEETS are rich in iron, which helps blood cells to be healthy and strong, and are effective for improving blood circulation; they can be helpful for treating menopausal disorders. Beets also help recovery of the liver, kidney, and gallbladder functions, and promote a healthy lymphatic system which can prevent the development of tumors and cancerous cells.

TEA

TEA

Tea is made by harvesting the tender leaves of the tea plant, drying them in a thick, cast iron pan over high heat, then repeating the drying and roasting process over and over. Drinking tea helps to enliven the body and clear the mind, and so it is greatly enjoyed by Buddhist practitioners especially while practicing asceticism and meditation. The culture of tea in Buddhist temples are grounded in the belief that tea drinking and spiritual practice are one (茶禪一味).

HOW TO DRINK TEA

1. Calm the mind and heart.
2. Boil the water completely to remove all cold elements.
3. Warm the teapot and tea cups by rinsing them with the boiled water.
4. Place the tea leaves inside the teapot and add the boiled water. When the tea is fully infused and the natural colors of the tea are visible, pour the tea into the cups.
5. Hold the cup in your hands. Observe the colors of the tea and enjoy the scent before taking a sip. Let the taste linger in your mouth, then swallow.
6. Feel the tea flowing down your throat, and the warmth spreading to all parts of your body. Being mindful of this sensation, enjoy the tea.

Dwaeji-gamja-cha

JERUSALEM ARTICHOKE TEA (SUNCHOKE TEA)

a full flavored tea that can be enjoyed by all with the added benefit of managing diabetes

Around the time in the spring when insects begin to stir (around March), I go to the foot of the mountains near Gameunsa Temple to dig up jerusalem artichokes (sunchokes) to make tea. I once gifted this jerusalem artichoke tea to a friend who suffers from diabetes. After drinking the tea regularly for 3 months, I heard that my friend's insulin levels have returned to normal and was incredibly grateful for the tea. With a caring and diligent heart, I recommend making homemade tea to care not only for your own health, but to share it with a generous heart for others as well.

Serves 4-5
Preparation time:
2 to 3 days

500 g jerusalem artichokes (sunchokes)
1 L of water

1. Wash jerusalem artichokes well, slice them into pieces 0.5 cm thick. Then, dry them thoroughly in shade.
   * When using a machine to dry the pieces, dry them completely in 50°C heat for 1 day, then sun-dry them for 1 hour.
2. Roast the dried jerusalem artichoke slices in a pan over low heat, then cool. Repeat 3 times.
3. Store in an airtight container.
4. **BOILING METHOD:** Boil 1 L of water and 20 g of jerusalem artichoke tea and brew for 20 to 30 minutes over medium heat.
5. **STEEPING METHOD:** Pour 200 ml of boiling water over 4 g of roasted jerusalem artichoke tea in a cup. Steep for 3 to 5 minutes.
6. Serve hot or cold.

JERUSALEM ARTICHOKES (SUNCHOKES) aid in controlling glucose levels in the body, is rich in dietary fibers, vitamins, and polyphenols, and also help break down body fat. The root vegetable also prevents osteoporosis by promoting bone health, and supports kidney functions to more effectively release bodily waste.

Hansang-charim

ONE TRAY SERVING

Each was good enough for a meal,
but together they became a well balanced whole.

PART 3

Stir-fried Brussels Sprouts with Crunchy Rice

Beet and Daikon Radish Pancake

Avocado Salad with Tofu

PART 4.

KNOW ONE, KNOW ALL
all life springs from the same root

POTATO

POTATO

The potato is rich in minerals like iron, potassium, and magnesium. It is also high in dietary fiber to improve intestinal health, as well as vitamin C to help the body recover from general fatigue. The skin of the potato contains immune boosting elements that prevent cancer and when consumed over time, this healthy vegetable promotes longevity.

Gamja-tarak-juk

MILKY POTATO PORRIDGE

savory and smooth, with a dash of indulgence

Serves 3-4
Preparation time: 5 minutes
Cooking time: 15 minutes

300 g potatoes, peeled and large diced (1 cm x 1 cm x 1 cm)
1 tablespoon perilla seed oil
3 tablespoons sticky rice flour (short-grain)
3 cups milk
1/2 cup water
1/2 teaspoon fine salt

1. Rinse off starch from the diced potatoes in water.
2. In a bowl, mix 1 cup of milk and sticky rice flour to make a slurry.
3. Heat the pot and add perilla seed oil. Add potato dices and sauté until translucent.
4. Add 2 cups of milk. Bring to a boil.
5. Add the flour slurry to the potatoes and reduce heat to low. Stir with a wooden spoon until soup is thickened.
6. Season with salt and serve.

Potatoes and milk are a great combination to supplement each other in terms of taste and nutrition. Milk softens the potato, enhances its taste and provides the proteins and fat components lacking in potato. Vitamin C and the rich fiber content of potatoes together with the lactose in milk, can help relieve constipation.

Gamja-bam-jorim

BRAISED POTATO AND CHESTNUT

a rich-tasting duo of chestnut and potato

Serves 3-4
Preparation time: 7 minutes
Cooking time: 15 minutes

300 g potatoes, peeled and cut to the same size as chestnuts

200 g chestnuts, peeled

1 tablespoon perilla seed oil

1 tablespoon roasted sesame seeds

1 tablespoon ginger juice

2 tablespoons grapeseed oil

2 tablespoons soy sauce

3 tablespoons rice syrup

1. Rinse the sliced potatoes and chestnuts in water.
2. Heat the pan and add grapeseed oil. Add potatoes to the pan and stir-fry until par-cooked.
3. Add the chestnuts and continue to stir-fry until both potatoes and chestnuts are translucent.
4. Add soy sauce and rice syrup. Stir-fry until evenly seasoned.
5. Add ginger juice and combine.
6. Turn off heat, add perilla seed oil and roasted sesame seeds. Stir well.
7. Plate and serve.

The flavor combination of the sweet chestnuts and mild potatoes blend harmoniously with each other. Other root vegetables like sweet potatoes, balloon flower roots, and deodeok (lance asiabell) can be substituted in place of the potatoes.

Gamja-pyogobeoseot-jjim

STEAMED STUFFED SHIITAKE MUSHROOMS WITH POTATO

doughy potato infused with the bold flavor of shiitake mushrooms

This dish is not only beautiful in presentation, but also very healthy and flavorful. It is perfect to serve as finger food at a party. Cooking by grilling is healthier than frying, but steaming is even healthier than grilling.

Serves 3-4
Preparation time: 15 minutes
Cooking time: 10 minutes

6 dried shiitake mushrooms, soaked in water and stems removed

300 g potatoes, finely grated

10 g cilantro, minced

1/2 teaspoon soy sauce

1/2 teaspoon fine salt

Ground black pepper to taste

1. Season mushrooms with soy sauce and black pepper.
2. Drain grated potatoes in a fine strainer to separate water from the solids. Reserve the two parts separately.
3. In approximately 3~5 minutes, the starch will begin to separate from the water. Discard water and save the starch.
4. In a mixing bowl, add the potato solids and starch. Season with fine salt and mix well.
5. Add minced cilantro to the mixture. Combine well.
6. Arrange the mushrooms so that the bottom side of mushroom caps face up.
7. Stuff the mushrooms with potato mixture.
8. After boiling water, steam the mushrooms for 10 minutes.
9. Plate and serve.

TOFU

TOFU

Tofu is full of healthy vegetable proteins. Eating tofu prevents the accumulation of harmful cholesterols in the body, and fatty acids in the blood and intestines. It promotes the growth of muscles and strengthens the bones, and even has anti-aging properties.

Dubu-eolkeun-jjigae

SPICY TOFU STEW

a piquant warmth that nourishes the soul

———

Serves 3-4
Preparation time: 5 minutes
Cooking time: 15 minutes

400 g tofu, firm, sliced (4 cm x 4 cm x 1 cm)

150 g enoki mushrooms

1 Korean green chili pepper, sliced on the bias

1 Korean red chili pepper, sliced on the bias

2 tablespoons Korean red chili powder

1 tablespoon perilla seed oil

1 tablespoon soy sauce

1 teaspoon ginger, minced

Fine salt to taste

4 cups vegetable stock

1. Trim the bottom part of the enoki mushrooms and tear them into small bunches about pencil width in thickness.
2. Heat the pot and add perilla seed oil.
3. Add Korean red chili powder and soy sauce. Sauté in low heat to make chili oil.
4. Add vegetable stock and bring to a boil.
5. Add tofu and bring back to a boil. Reduce heat and simmer until tofu is well seasoned.
6. Add minced ginger and enoki mushrooms. Bring to a boil again.
7. Add sliced chili peppers and adjust seasoning with salt. Serve hot.

———

This stew may a little bit too spicy to enjoy as an everyday meal, but it provides a much needed boost to the immune system when you are feeling ill or with a cold.

Dubu-jangajji

PICKLED TOFU

protein packed in pureness

————

Serves 6-12
Preparation time: 40 minutes
Cooking time: 3 days

1 kg tofu, firm, sliced 2 cm thick

3 tablespoons grapeseed oil

1/2 cup soy sauce

3 cups water

30 g ginger, peeled and sliced thinly

5 dried chili peppers

2 pieces dried kelp (5 cm x 5 cm)

1 tablespoon fine salt

1. Pat dry tofu slices and sprinkle with salt.
2. Heat the pan and add grapeseed oil.
3. Pan-fry tofu slices until golden brown on both sides.
4. In a pot, add water, soy sauce, dried chili peppers, ginger, and kelp. Simmer over medium heat for about 30 minutes. Strain and cool.
5. In a separate container, arrange the tofu slices and pour in the pickling liquid.
6. Cover and leave in room temperature for 2 to 3 days.
7. After 2 to 3 days, drain the pickling liquid, add it to a pot and bring to a boil. Cool down.
8. Pour the cooled pickling liquid to container with the tofu again.
9. Use a plate to push down the tofu into the liquid, making sure to keep all tofu slices submerged under the liquid.
10. Repeat steps 7, 8, and 9.
11. Cover and refrigerate to store.

————

Whenever we make handmade tofu at the temple, we always pickle some of it with soybean paste or soy sauce. People think it is difficult to pickle tofu since they are very soft, but with this simplified recipe you can easily make and preserve pickled tofu for quite a long time: First, fry the tofu crisp with oil and pour lukewarm boiled soy sauce over them. After 3 or 4 days, filter the soy sauce only and boil it again. Pour the cooled down soy sauce onto tofu and repeat this procedure twice more.

Dubu-ueong-jorim

BRAISED TOFU AND BURDOCK ROOT

a pleasant balance of crunch and silkiness

___

Serves 3-4
Preparation time: 10 minutes
Cooking time: 20 minutes

300 g tofu, firm, sliced (4 cm x 4 cm x 1 cm)

300 g burdock roots, peeled and fine julienned

3 Korean green chili peppers, seeded and fine julienned

2 tablespoons perilla seed oil

2 tablespoons rice syrup

1 tablespoon soy sauce

1 tablespoon fermented green plum extract

2 tablespoons grapeseed oil

1/2 teaspoon fine salt

1 tablespoon black sesame seeds

1. Score an "X" on one side of the tofu slices with a paring knife.
2. Pat dry tofu slices and sprinkle with salt.
3. Heat the pan and add grapeseed oil.
4. Pan-fry tofu slices until golden brown on both sides. Take the tofu slices out and set aside.
5. In another pan, add perilla seed oil and burdock root, and stir-fry well.
6. Add soy sauce, rice syrup and fermented green plum extract to the roots. Cook over low heat until burdock root is well seasoned.
7. Add tofu slices and stir gently together. Turn off heat.
8. Add julienned chili peppers and black sesame seeds. Stir gently to mix.
9. Plate and serve.

___

This dish is a deliciously well-balanced combination of the soft tofu with the crunch of the burdock roots. We tend to swallow soft foods without chewing them very much; if the dish incorporates a little bit of crunch, not only does it add to the playful textures, but it makes us chew and swallow it more carefully.

TOMATO

TOMATO

Rich in vitamins and minerals, the tomato is an alkaline food. The red lycopene in tomatoes gets rid of free oxygen radicals, acting as a great antioxidant for the body. The levels of lycopene increase even more when cooked. Tomatoes also contain rutin, which strengthens blood vessels and lowers blood pressure.

Tomato-bibim-myeon

COLD NOODLES WITH TOMATO DRESSING

an appetizing concoction of sweet and tart

This recipe was made right after I made a variant of this dish: mixed cold noodles with strawberry dressing. Even though it is a very simple recipe, it is well balanced in nutrients and pleasing in taste. If you make the dressing in advance, it will become even more delicious as the fermentation process will augment the flavors. Coated with the tomato dressing, the cold noodles will not soften or get mushy quickly, which makes it suitable to be served even over longer periods of time or at larger events.

Serves 3-4
Preparation time: 10 minutes
Cooking time: 10 minutes

---

160 g Korean thin wheat noodles
60 g baby sprouts, washed and dried
8 cups water
Coarse salt to taste

TOMATO DRESSING:
400 g tomatoes
2 tablespoons fermented green plum extract
2 tablespoons perilla seed oil
1 tablespoon soy sauce
1 tablespoon organic sugar
1 tablespoon sesame seeds, ground
Fine salt to taste

1. Cut a small "X" mark on top of tomatoes.
2. Blanch tomatoes in water until their skin starts to peel.
3. Shock tomatoes in ice water and peel the skin.
4. Cut them into quarters and remove the cores. Puree in a blender coarsely.
5. In a mixing bowl, add tomato puree, fermented green plum extract, perilla seed oil, soy sauce, organic sugar, and grounded sesame seeds. Mix well.
6. Add salt to boiling water, then add Korean thin wheat noodles and cook.
7. Drain and rinse with cold water to rinse off the starch and to cool the noodles. Drain well.
8. Toss thin wheat noodles with the tomato dressing.
9. Add baby sprouts and toss. Serve cold.

Bangul-tomato-gaji-jorim

BRAISED EGGPLANT WITH CHERRY TOMATOES

the marriage of flavors are enhanced the more you chew

───────

Serves 3-4
Preparation time: 5 minutes
Cooking time: 10 minutes

12 cherry tomatoes

2 Asian eggplants, cut into 4 cm long pieces

1 Korean cheongyang green chili pepper, seeded and minced

* May be substituted with serrano chili peppers

1 tablespoon perilla seed oil

2 tablespoons soy sauce

1 tablespoon rice syrup

1/2 cup vegetable stock

1. Slit the eggplant pieces in quarters with one end still intact.
   * Do not cut all the way through.
2. In a pan, add perilla seed oil and eggplants, and stir-fry well.
3. Add vegetable stock, soy sauce, and rice syrup. Stir well to mix.
4. Cover and braise the eggplants in medium heat for about 2 to 3 minutes.
5. When eggplants are tender, add cherry tomatoes and cook through.
6. Sprinkle minced chili pepper and serve.

───────

I came up with this recipe when one of my neighborhood farmers brought me a large bundle of eggplants from his field. Since it is hard to preserve eggplants for a long period of time, I braised them well with this soy sauce seasoning. During this process, I found that the tenderness of eggplants really added to the flavors, and a new recipe was created.

Put-tomato-jangajji

PICKLED GREEN TOMATOES

a mouthful of crunch and vigor

Serves 6-12
Preparation time: 30 minutes
Cooking time: 4 days

1 kg green tomatoes, cored, quartered, and sliced into thick pieces

* If tomatoes are small, cut into halves

1 cup soy sauce

1 cup water

1 cup vinegar

1 cup fermented green plum extract

1/2 cup organic sugar

1. In a pot, add soy sauce, water, and sugar. Bring to a boil.
2. Add vinegar and fermented green plum extract. Turn off the heat.
3. In a container, arrange the green tomatoes and pour the pickling liquid over them.
4. Use a plate to push the tomatoes down, making sure that they are all submerged under the liquid.
5. Cover and leave in room temperature for 3~4 days.
6. After 3~4 days drain the pickling liquid, add it to a pot and boil. Cool down.
7. Pour the cooled pickling liquid back in the container with green tomatoes.
8. Repeat steps 5, 6, and 7.
9. Cover and refrigerate to store.

I used unripe green tomatoes to pickle after all the well-ripened tomatoes were harvested. After the fermentation and pickling process, the green tomatoes become uniquely special with its distinct tomato aromas. Unripe pickled tomatoes retain a crunch and their flavors can even last for several years.

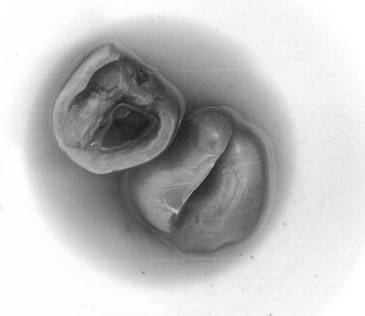

Hansang-charim

ONE TRAY SERVING

Each was good enough for a meal,
but together they became a well balanced whole.

PART 4

Milky Potato Porridge

Braised Tofu and Burdock Root

Pickled Green Tomatoes

INDEX

ACKNOWLEDGEMENTS

The clear blue sky and a cool refreshing wind welcomed me when I arrived in New York and stepped outside the airport.

I visited a farmer's market when I visited Manhattan, in hopes of introducing ways to incorporate the flavors and seasonings of Korean temple food while using local ingredients. I was honestly struck by the ingredients I found: the organic vegetables, lovingly cared for by the farmers, retained their freshness, and the aroma of the mushrooms still echoed the scent of the woods. It was not only an educational experience for me, but also a surprising one. I had thought that in such an urban setting, fast foods and packaged foods would be overwhelmingly prevalent, and fresh, organic ingredients more difficult to find. I was so happy to see how fresh organic foods were readily accessible for all.

First of all, I want to thank each and every farmer who works so hard to produce such beautiful ingredients. Knowing that these vegetables and foods can be found in the city gave me such a happiness and hope as I became certain that I could share the true flavors and spirit of Korean temple food through my recipes. It is my most sincere hope that many people will be able to learn the healthy cooking methods of temple food and that it can contribute to the overall wellness of both mind and body.

Many people joined me on this path in creating this book of Korean temple food. I would like to thank Chef Youngsun Lee and Jessica Jung Choi who have worked with me with such enthusiasm in expressing these recipes in English, and to James SJ Ryu, Kate Kim, and Sun Jeon who have been incredibly helpful with the detailed aspects of the translations, and to Mickey Yoon-Jung Hyun for her work in the editing process.

I would also like to express my gratitude to the Venerable Il Yeo, Venerable Geun Beom, Venerable Bo Moon, Jongnam Heo, Chef Yi Yung Liu, Chef Gu Jin-Kwang, Hyeonja Park, and Soohyun Kim for their ongoing support, as well as photographer Dukgwan Moon for all his beautiful work for this book and ceramic artist Daeseop Kwon for his elegant pieces.

Finally, I would like to thank all of those based here in New York who have worked so hard to help this book come into being: Kuki Hee-Yeon Sohn, Creative Director of SRC&C, Hung Kyung Lee, President of ICP Inc., and Jeong K. Kim, President of Korean Buddhist Culture Services in New York. I am most humbly grateful to you all.

To everyone who has taken on this journey with me, in remembrance of your generous merit and charity, I pray that you are always with serenity in your mind, peace within your soul, happiness in your heart, and oneness with the way.

WOOKWAN entered the Yaksusa temple in the Gwanak Mountains in 1988 under the teaching of the Venerable Jeong Hwa. She graduated from Suwon Bongnyeongsa Sangha University where she also completed research work. She received her master's degree in Buddhist studies and completed her doctoral coursework at the University of Delhi in India; afterwards, she practiced vipasanna meditation in Myanmar and its vicinities.

In September of 2010, Wookwan participated in the first Korean Temple Food Festival held in New York City. The event was extremely well received by the local audience. Following, in October of 2014, she held a lecture and tasting at a Slow Food event held in Turin, Italy, and in 2015 went to Spain to represent Korea at Madrid Fusion 2015 to demonstrate Korean temple food and traditional barley red chili paste; she also held a workshop of temple food at the Korean Cultural Center in Spain.

In August 2016, with invitation from the Korean Cultural Center Kazakhstan, Wookwan presented a temple food workshop, and the following summer in 2017, hosted an exhibition and luncheon event at the Korean Cultural Center in Hungary. December of 2017, she was invited by the Korean Cultural Center New York to hold a special lecture and workshop in partnership with the Natural Gourmet Institute and the Culinary Tech Center.

Within Korea, Wookwan has held numerous lectures and programs hosted by the official educational sector of the Cultural Corps of Korean Buddhism under the Jogye Order of Korean Buddhism since 2010, and in 2015, she has actively taken part in workshops and teaching events hosted by the Ministry of Agriculture, Food and Rural Affairs and the Korean Food Promotion Institute. As the Director of the Mahayeon Temple Food Cultural Center in Icheon, Korea, she holds regular workshops on temple food and also hosts events in partnership with Gyeonggi Province and Icheon City.

Published works include "*Wookwan Sunim's Temple Food with a Mother's Touch*" and "*Wookwan Sunim's The Taste of Awakening*" in Korean. You can follow her on Instagram @wookwansunim.

I have been a chef at many commercial kitchens ranging from casual dining, food trucks, and vegetarian restaurants to upscale fine dining establishments, but no matter where I was, there were always two factors that brought me the most pressure. These two things were "taste" and "money." These two factors that drive the modern food industry were pulling me away from my true passion for food.

As I was getting to know Wookwan and her cooking, she challenged me to think about my philosophy for food. After agonizing for quite some time, I came to the conclusion that I wanted to make food that was both "good" and "right." I believe that healthy eating does not just come from eating luxurious or fancy foods, but rather it comes from not eating things that are harmful for the body. This is because any food can be either good or bad for you, depending on your bodily needs or how the dish is cooked.

Living in the modern era, our palates are exposed to an overwhelming range of flavors and tastes, and we often forget to feel the food, nor do we yearn for true, simple flavors from ingredients. We have often forgotten how to listen to what our body needs, not what our tongues crave.